Mommy, I Can't Sit Still!

Coping With Hyperactive and Aggressive Children

By

K. Daniel O'Leary

New Horizon Press
Publishers

Library of Congress Cataloging in Publication Data

O'Leary, K. Daniel, 1940-
   Mommy, I can't sit still!

   Bibliography: p.
   Includes index.
   1. Hyperactive child syndrome. 2. Aggressiveness in
children. I. Title.
RJ506.H9044   1984   616.85'89   84-2104
ISBN 0-88282-000-1

Manufactured in the United States of America

PERMISSIONS

The figure "Stimulant medication and eye-hand coordination in hyperkinesis" is reprinted by permission of the publisher from the article "Using the Antihyperkinesis Agents" which appeared in *Patient Care®* Magazine. Copyright © 1978. Patient Care Communications, Inc., Darien, Conn. All Rights Reserved.

The ATRS is reprinted by permission of C. Keith Conners.

The editorial, "The Violence Stays On When the TV Goes Off," is reprinted by permission from *Newsday*. © Newsday, Inc.

The quotation from Aggression in the Schools by Dan Olweus is reprinted by permission of Hemisphere Publishing Corporation, New York, NY.

The quotation on page 15 is from Winston Churchill, *My Early Life: A Roving Commission*. © Copyright 1930 Charles Scribner's Sons; copyright renewed 1958 Winston Churchill. Used with permission of Charles Scribner's Sons.

ACKNOWLEDGMENTS

Susan Geiss provided excellent editorial and substantive feedback to me throughout the writing of this book. Her aid was outstanding.

Dedication

This book is dedicated to the Octorara Area School in Chester County, Pennsylvania. The Octorara Area School and a number of people in the towns in that beautiful rural Chester County area, now made famous by the painter Andrew Wyeth, were very special to me, my brother Brian, and my mother. The towns, Cochranville, Atglen, Parkesburg, and Christiana, and the farms nearby have always held a very special place in my heart. Most important, the warmth and support of many people in those towns and farms enabled me to escape the childhood and adolescent problems of aggression and hyperactivity described in this book.

Contents

Foreword

How can we help the hyperactive or aggressive child to realize his or her true potential, to function as a productive, caring individual in our world? This is the question parents, mental health professionals and teachers are seeking to answer as the number of children with these behavioral and emotional difficulties seems to rise alarmingly. Yet L.H. Cohen described this kind of childhood disability in detail over twenty years ago and used the term "organic driven-ness" to denote the apparent surplus of inner compulsion and lack of outer constraints which characterize these childrens' behavior. Is there a pervading reason why we are seeing so much more of this problem today? Is life too complicated? Are we too demanding or critical or just more psychologically aware?

Many books have been written by child psychologists and experts attempting to solve the problem of maladjusted children. These books tend to approach the problem from either the professional view or the parental view. Both are justified but incomplete. This author believes a threefold approach is necessary if we are to understand fully and deal with hyperactivity and aggressiveness. The first is a thorough assessment of the child's perceptions, observations and feelings about the environment in which he or she lives. The second is a review of the history, causes and description of the problem through the eyes of parents and professionals. The third is a complete assessment and review of the most up to date pharmacological, dietary and psychological treatments and where help can be found.

Such a book which chronicles problem behavior as poor attention span, distractability, impulsivity, poor coordination, learning difficulties and family hardships can seem designed to discourage, make uncomfortable or frighten those who must deal with such problem behavior, but just the opposite should be true.

We must realize that hyperactivity and aggressiveness is not just one but a cluster of symptoms ranging from minimal to

1

maximum. And we must realize that there is a record of encouraging medical and psychological treatments of which one or a combination may give you the help and encouragement to deal successfully with the behavioral and emotional difficulties of the hyperactive or aggressive child in your life.

This book was written for the general public, and I felt that parents and teachers of children with problems of aggression and hyperactivity were the specific people to whom I was talking. The book was designed to provide a clear understanding of the causes and treatment for the problems. It is not a "cook book," with particular recipes to follow, but rather a complete digest of available help. To provide optimal amounts of sources for treatment and behavioral change, a special chapter is included on the how, where and when to locate aid. In that chapter a potential consumer of professional services is alerted to the best ways to select psychotherapists, physicians, and educational specialists who may have special knowledge of the problems of hyperactive and aggressive children.

This book should also serve as a source book for any professional dealing with children who have problems of aggression and hyperactivity since all of the important causes and treatments for such children are discussed in its pages.

As our knowledge progresses, the outlook for such children becomes increasingly hopeful and as we put this knowledge to work in better treatment and more understanding, improvements at every level—personal, family and educational—will be seen.

Introduction

Children's Feelings About Themselves and Their Problems

As concerned onlookers, we parents, friends, teachers and professionals see hyperactive and hyperaggressive children in relation to the so called normal patterns of our own world. But it is in the self perceptions of such maladjusted children that clues are to be found about their feelings, perceptions and observations. Perhaps the most penetrating of these insights may be found in their own words and drawings about themselves and their lives.

Confusion About Reasons for Their Behavior

Aggressive noncompliant children are often confused about why they behave as they do. Consider the following case of a ten-year-old boy who was very aggressive verbally with his father, mother and brother, but he was not seen as aggressive by his teacher.

The self-descriptions are taken from my consultations with this ten-year-old boy, Sean, regarding a visit to his father's house. His parents were separated for approximately one year.

Dr. O'Leary: Why did you keep turning the television off when you were visiting your father this weekend?

Sean: He was watching football. I don't like it, and I wanted him to take me to buy me an ice cream cone.

Dr. O'Leary: When you kept turning off the TV, what did your dad do?

Sean: First he hit me, and then he told me he'd take me home if I didn't stop.

Dr. O'Leary: Did you stop?

Sean: No.

Dr. O'Leary: Did your dad take you home?

3

Self-drawing of Normal Boy.
Note relaxed expression. (Same size as original drawing).

Self-Drawing of Hyperactive Boy

As is evident from the skates, this hyperactive boy clearly sees himself in action. Note unusual delineation of eyes and bared teeth. (Same size as original drawing).

Sean: Yes, and then he and my mother argued because
                   she wanted to be free to go to visit a friend.

Sean would change from week to week about whether he
wanted to go to his father's. He would dream about going there
and having a good time. He confided in me that he wanted to
have a good time with his father, but that he simply could not
get along with him. He knew his aggressive behavior would
bring his visitation to a halt, yet he frequently displayed such
tantrums.

In short, Sean was confused about why he behaved as he did.
He often wanted to please his father and to have a good time
with him on his visitation, but he would also get angry at his
father when he had known that his father argued with his mother.

Denial of Problems

Aggressive behavior of either a verbal or physical nature is
often very unpredictable; it may often occur only every three or
four weeks in an aggressive teenager, but when it occurs it seems
irrational and out of character. The occasional nature of the
aggressive behavior, however, can lead an adolescent to feel that
he really does not have any significant problems. Consider the
actions of a 14-year-old boy, Jay, who was expelled from public
school and who was later kicked out of two private schools. The
boy's parents are both professionals, and he has two brothers
and a sister. The brothers and sister do very well in school. Jay
does average work in school in general, but he often excels in
language and social studies. In fact, he is in an advanced social
studies class. He is a short, stocky boy who is often teased about
his size. I saw him on the first occasion after he had threatened
a school mate with a switch blade.

Dr. O'Leary: How have things been going during the past
             week?
Jay: Fine, no problem.
Dr. O'Leary: Did any kids tease you this week?
Jay: No, not really.

Dr. O'Leary: Did you get angry at anyone?

Jay: No.

Dr. O'Leary: (After about a 15 minute discussion). It seems that things have been going quite well with you during the past week. Before we stop, however, I'd like to talk with you and your mother together.

Dr. O'Leary: Mrs. Stern, from what Jay tells me things have been going quite well in the past week. How do you view things?

Mrs. Stern: Jay has generally been quite good. He studies each night and he hasn't had any fights with his older brother. Last week I was frightened by one incident. Some old "friends" of his took his bike and hid it over the weekend. Jay was enraged by this, and when he saw them come up the driveway on Monday, he ran out of the house with a sledge hammer. He was uncontrollably shaking. I literally had to restrain him.

This incident, like other intermittent incidents of rage, have led to school expulsions and nasty fights with neighbors.

Jay "forgets" about negative interactions with others, even though he knows that I will talk with his mother at each visit after seeing him. He never denies that incidents related by his mother occur, and the infrequency of the negative events in part contributes to his poor reporting of events. Most importantly, they also prompt him at times to feel that he doesn't have a very significant problem.

Saying Things They Don't Mean

Most children who are hyperactive also have problems with low frustration tolerance and feeling that they have to have their demands easily met.

Alex was a 14-year-old boy who had been on medication for hyperactivity since he was eight years old. He was described as hyperactive since infancy. When he was two years old he was seen as stubborn, needing very little sleep and independent. His school record in junior high school was average, though his intelligence tests indicated that he had superior intelligence. Fortunately, he asked to come to see me, and he described himself this way on his first visit.

Alex: I want help dealing with my bad behavior. When I am out of control I say things I don't mean. I do many things without thinking.

Dr. O'Leary: What kind of mean things do you do?

Alex: I go after my brother (two years younger). I stand outside his bedroom door and tell him that he stinks and that he is a poindexter. . . . Sometimes we fight pretty hard when my parents are away. I just can't let him alone. He is my best friend sometimes, but other times we fight.

Basically, Alex could not stand being alone in his room for long periods, and he would literally harass his brother when his parents were away. He had a similar problem in school; he would call out answers in class or ask questions without being called upon. His teachers described him as immature and occasionally he would be asked to leave the class. Upon coming to visit me, his parents were considering whether to send him to a special school to prevent fights between Alex and his brother.

Blaming Others For Their Problems

For many aggressive and hyperactive children, the predominant experience appears to be one of failure and the negative evaluations that come from peers, parents, siblings and teachers. When the children talk about their problems in a general way, they are often in agreement with their parents about what needs to be changed. That is, they recognize how their actions are viewed by others and appear to accept some responsibility for the unhappiness in their lives. For example, the following lists were developed independently by Charley and his mother:

Charley's list of:

What Mom should change:	What Charley should change:
1. Yell less	1. Listen with no backtalk
2. Trust me more (don't always say, "I bet you did it")	2. Keep bedroom neat
3. Wash clothes regularly	3. Fight less with other kids
4. Lose weight	

What Mom Should change:	What Charley should change:
1. Pick on him less	1. Don't always have the last word—no backtalk
2. Be more positive	2. Do considerate things for others
3. Make him feel more wanted	

Clearly, Charley and his mother concurred about what many of the problems were and what needed changing. Charley did not view himself as a victim of a world that heaped failure at his feet. However, when Charley was talking about a particularly problematic incident that happened during the previous week, he lost his perspective and experienced the situation primarily as caused by someone else.

Dr. O'Leary: I understand you were involved in a fight during lunch. What happened?

Charley: A bunch of those jerks were hanging around talking about us (kids in the special education class). They walked over and started up with us.

Dr. O'Leary: What did you do?

Charley: Shoved one guy up against the lockers; what do you think I was supposed to do?

Dr. O'Leary: How did they start up with you?

Charley: You know, they were going to gang up on us; we had to protect ourselves.

Dr. O'Leary: Did they actually do anything?

Charley: Sure they did. I know if they kept looking at us that way, they'd start something. But we showed them. Now they know not to start fights with us.

Dr. O'Leary: But why did you get in trouble?

Charley: The aide—she said we started it. They always say that even if it was the other guys' fault. They don't like us either.

Dr. O'Leary: Could you have done anything to keep the fight from happening?

Charley: No. They started it. They made me mad and when I'm mad, I can't help it!

In Charley's opinion, this was just another example of how he was treated unfairly and had no alternative and no responsibility.

Feelings About Medication

Tom, a nine-year-old hyperactive boy, came to school one morning without his medication. He completed less than half the work he usually accomplished, was very disruptive in class, and got into two fights at recess. Tom's teacher, Mr. C., had the following conversation with him.

Mr. C.: Tom, what happened today? You got hardly any work done and the lunch aide told me you were fighting with Brad and Michael.

Tom: My mother couldn't get my pills from the hospital—my pills make me get done with the work. Besides, you give too much work. How do you expect anybody to finish all that? And I didn't start the fights!

Mr. C.: Wait a minute. Tell me what happened.

Tom: They . . . they were pushing in line—trying to hurt me (becomes teary).

Mr. C.: Calm down. Let's talk about it. I saw you coming down the hall. You were pushing too.

Tom: No I wasn't!! It was my turn to be first!

Mr. C.: But that's not something to get so angry about.

Tom: I can't help it. I get angry without my pill. I can't do anything right—it's not fair! (crying, banging his books around).

Tom's reactions are fairly typical of children who show a strong positive response to psychostimulant medication. Without it, they feel victimized, tend to place blame on others and will not accept responsibility, have difficulty controlling their anger, and express a dependency on the medication. When they are receiving their medication, they feel calmer and less emotional and feel they have a good chance of meeting the expectations of their teachers.

Feelings of Bullies

Bullies, or boys who harass others in mental and physical ways are common in all schools. Their behavior is remarkably stable over a several year period in elementary school. They are physically stronger than the average child. They feel tough, and they feel confident, and they find a target. Consider the following picture.

"If there is . . . . a potential passive whipping boy in the class—anxious, insecure, fearful of being assertive and aggressive, and often physically weak as well, he will be discovered by the bully. He is the weak link in the chain, the one who does not retaliate when he is attacked, who becomes afraid and perhaps cries, who is unwilling or unable to ward off attacks by even fairly harmless antagonists. Generally, he disapproves of taking part in rough games with the other boys of the class. He also feels rather alone and isolated.

"For a boy with bullying tendencies, the potential whipping boy is an ideal target. His anxiousness, defenselessness, and crying give the bully a marked feeling of superiority and supremacy, also a sort of satisfaction of vague revengeful impul-

ses'' (Olweus, p. 142, 1978). In contrast to other boys, bullies
feel that "fighting is the best way to solve conflicts," that they
"would like to become boxer(s)," and that one should (not) be
nice to those who are younger and weaker than they are (Olweus,
p. 107, 1978).

Positive Feelings About Channeling Energy

Mark was a 12-year-old boy who would frequently swear at
his brother and who would use obscene gestures to his mother,
usually behind her back but occasionally in front of her. He was
quite intelligent but he had never received very good grades in
school. His mother and father cared for him a great deal, but
they were extremely frustrated at his emotional outbursts. Nonetheless, he could occasionally display periods of excellent control of his behavior for seven-to-ten days. One week when he
did this, he came into the office beaming. When I asked him
what he did to control himself he had the following comments:

Dr. O'Leary: How did you control your behavior so well this
week?

Mark: You challenged me to see if I could do it, and
I wanted to show you and Mom and Dad that
I could do it . . . I also knew that if I didn't
shape up soon they wouldn't let me go on the
class trip to New York City. I avoided my
brother as much as possible.

Dr. O'Leary: Did you take my suggestion to spend more time
with some of your friends after school?

Mark: Yea, on two days I went to Dan's place, and
we rode dirt bikes. We had an extra band practice on Wednesday after school so I didn't spend
any time with my brother Wednesday. The other
times I just tried to keep busy with the Atari.

Dr. O'Leary: You sound like you feel pretty good about what
you did.

Mark: I know I can control myself if I really want to.
It just seems like a tough job a lot of the time.

For many children with problems of aggression and hyper-activity know they can control their behavior some of the time, and they feel good about their periodic success at controlling their own behavior. It does take effort, however, and it takes more effort for most of these children and adolescents than it did for you and me when we were in elementary and junior high school. They need more help to exert this control, and they certainly need more positive support for their efforts.

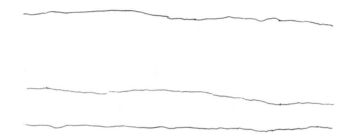

Slow Drawing of Three Lines
Children with emotional and behavioral problems, especially problems of impulse control find it hard to draw these lines slowly. As is clear from these lines, the boy made many starts and stops as he went across the page. (Reduced to 38 percent of original size).

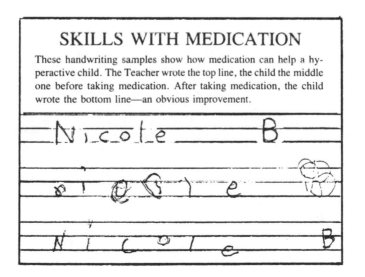

SKILLS WITH MEDICATION
These handwriting samples show how medication can help a hyperactive child. The Teacher wrote the top line, the child the middle one before taking medication. After taking medication, the child wrote the bottom line—an obvious improvement.

1

Description of Aggressive and Hyperactive Children

I was now seven years old, and I was what grown-up people in their offhand way called a "troublesome boy." It appeared that I was to go away from home for many weeks at a stretch in order to do lessons under masters. (p. 8)

The school my parents selected for my education was one of the most fashionable and expensive in the country. It modelled itself upon Eton (a fashionable private school) and aimed at being preparatory for that Public School above all others. It was supposed to be the very latest thing in schools. Only ten boys in a class; electric lights (then a wonder); a swimming pond; spacious football and cricket grounds. How I hated this school, and what a life of anxiety I lived there for more than two years. I made very little progress at my lessons, and none at all at games. I counted the days and hours to the end of every term, when I should return home from this hateful servitude and range my soldiers in line of battle on the nursery floor. (p. 12)

I had scarcely passed my twelfth birthday when I entered the inhospitable regions of examinations, through which for the next seven years I was destined to journey. These examinations were a great trial to me. The subjects which were dearest to the examiners were almost invariably those I fancied least. I would have liked to have been examined in history, poetry and writing essays. The examiners, on the other hand, were partial to Latin and mathematics. All their will prevailed. Moreover, the questions which they asked in both these subjects were almost invariably those to which I was unable to suggest a satisfactory answer. I should have liked to be asked to say what I knew. They always tried to ask what I did not know. When I should have willingly displayed my knowledge, they sought to expose my ignorance. This sort of treatment had only one result: I did not do well in examinations. (from Winston Churchill's autobiography, *My Early Life: A Roving Commission* (1930) p. 15.)

15

Churchill was a boy with academic and behavioral problems, and at the age of nine he was removed from school because of his difficulties. His childhood behavior was described by biographers as intractible, stubborn, spoiled, unpromising. Today, he would be called a "conduct problem."

The most common psychological problems of children who are referred to mental health clinics are aggression and hyperactivity. Listen to several parents' descriptions of such children to psychologists, psychiatrists, and social workers:

"My boy is always fighting with other kids; he is a bully, and he has a chip on his shoulder. He seems to feel my husband and I don't care for him as much as we do for his brothers and sisters."

"My ten-year-old boy won't do what I ask him to do unless I threaten him severely; I sometimes wonder whether he has a hearing problem. He refuses to do his homework, yet he is barely passing. I could handle his problems before he went to school, but since first grade he has become unbearable. Now my husband and I argue about how to discipline him, and he is affecting our marriage."

"My boy has been a terror since he was able to walk; he was always pulling things from my drawers and cabinets. He never seems able to sit still; he is up and down at the dinner table. He had difficulty learning to print and write, and now he is beginning to fall behind in reading. His teacher feels we should check with a neurologist to see if he has some minor brain damage. What frustrates me most is that all his teachers feel he is a bright lad."

"My daughter is 12 years old. She uses foul language at home but does not use such language at school or when we are with friends; she is surly with me but is usually afraid to be disobedient with her dad. She is beginning to drink and smoke with her friends, and she has begun to hide cigarettes in her drawers. She has a pretty face but is a little overweight, and she feels self-conscious about her appearance."

We hear such examples every day as we listen to parents' woeful tales about interactions with their children. Boys were described in three of the four above examples, and boys with such problems appear in clinics about three to four times as often as girls. Some of the problems were apparent in these children when they were as young as one year old, but most became obvious when the children entered school. No outstanding physical problems were noted, but one child had poor coordination which led some teachers to think that the child may have had some minor brain damage or dysfunction. Similarly, most children who come to mental health clinics do not have any clear physical defects or abnormalities. The central issue is that the child does not comply with parental or teacher requests. Such children have long been called conduct problems, but other labels, such as hyperactivity, aggression, minimal brain dysfunction, and attentional deficit, are fairly commonly used by professionals.

The important point to note now is that aggression and hyperactivity are the most frequent of all types of childhood problems. They are especially serious because they often are followed by later adult problems, such as alcoholism, difficulty maintaining a job, and legal infractions. In fact, studies of adults who as children attended mental health clinics show that childhood aggression is a greater predictor of adult problems than any other type of childhood problem (e.g., anxiety, shyness, bedwetting). Aggression and hyperactivity generally occur together although it is not uncommon for a child to be either aggressive or hyperactive. Aggressive, demanding, impulsive, academically deficient, learning disabled, and hyperactive are labels often given to children with problems of aggression and hyperactivity.

Aggressive. The outstanding feature of children with problems of hyperactivity and aggression is that they often fight, hit, or are assaultive. In every large-scale study conducted of children's behavior problems (Quay, 1979), the first feature that stands out among all others is aggression in one form or another, either verbal or physical. That is, when parents, teachers, or mental health professionals rate children's emotional adjustment, aggression has a greater impact on the adults' ratings than any other characteristic of children's behavior.

Physical aggression in a preschool child usually involves hit-and-run attacks on brothers, sisters, or playmates. It is often associated with an inability to communicate well about sharing toys or to a lack of understanding about rules of certain games. Physical aggression in a preschool child can be highly infrequent yet cause grave problems because the children are often unaware of the consequences of their actions. For example, a child in my son's nursery school class fractured my child's nose as he intentionally hit him with a baseball bat. Of course, I presume that the child who hit my son had no knowledge that his actions would have such an impact.

In an elementary school child, aggression is seen in verbal attacks against students and teachers (e.g., "Johnny, you're a fat slob"; "Mrs. Brown, you run this class like a military school, and it stinks.") Aggression is also seen in physical acts against others (e.g., hitting and poking) and in acts of anger directed toward school property (using knives to slit or mutilate furniture, clogging urinals or toilets, and breaking windows). In the home, aggression is seen most frequently in talking back to parents or hitting brothers, sisters, and even occasionally pets.

The bully who picks on smaller children is a well known phenomenon in almost every junior high and high school. Harassment, teasing, exclusion from games, and unexpected hitting are all part of the scene in which one or two children become the target of a bully's aggression. This phenomenon has been depicted by the Scandinavian psychologist, Olweus, as "Bullies and Whipping Boys." In his book, *Aggression in the Schools* (1978), Olweus presented the results of a major study of "mobbing" or aggressive gang activities against a target. He studied approximately 1,000 boys between the ages of 12 and 16 years and his clinical description of the "Whipping Boy and Bully Problems" follows:

> Among the boys in a class, there are normally some conflicts and tensions of different kinds. Usually there are also many slight aggressive interactions, partly for fun, as a form of self-assertion and for the testing out of strength relations among the boys. If there is a potential bully (or several) in such a group, this will influence the boys' activities. The interactions will be rougher, more vehement and violent. The irascible temperament of the bully, his marked needs to assert himself, to dominate and subdue others, make themselves strongly felt. Even minor adversities and frustrations lead to intense reactions, which often assume an aggressive form because of his inclination to use violent means in conflicts. Due to the physical strength of the bully, his aggressive attacks are often unpleasant and painful to others. Even if he prefers to attack the weakest boys, whom he is certain of defeating, he is also not afraid of starting fights with other boys in the class. Generally, he feels rather tough and self-confident.
>
> If there is also a potential passive whipping boy in the class—anxious, insecure, fearful of being assertive and aggressive, and often physically weak as well—he will soon be discovered by the bully. He is the weak link in the chain, the one who does not retaliate when he is attacked, who becomes afraid and perhaps cries, who is unwilling or unable to ward off attacks by even fairly harmless antagonists. Generally, he disapproves of taking part in rough games with the other boys of the class. He also feels rather alone and isolated.
>
> For a boy with bullying tendencies, the potential whipping boy is an ideal target. His anxiousness, defenselessness, and crying give the bully a marked feeling of superiority and supremacy, also a sort of satisfaction of vague revengeful impulses.
>
> But the bully usually wants to have others join him, and he soon induces his closest friends to pick on the whipping boy. There is always something in the looks, clothing, or manners of the whipping boy that can be attacked. Often, it is equally pleasant for the bully to see other boys harass the whipping boy as to do it himself. And after all, he keeps a line of retreat open, if there should be unpleasant consequences. But the adults at school frequently do not pay attention to the fuss, or they are not in the vicinity and let the boys themselves settle their conflicts. (p. 142)

While one may have great sympathy for the whipping boys

described above, the bullies also have their share of serious problems, for their aggressive behavior is often reflective of an extremely insecure and troubled individual.

Demanding. The words, "I Want What I Want When I Want It," from the song, *Mademoiselle Modiste* by Henry Blossom, aptly describe children with problems of aggression and hyperactivity. The child will press his/her parents or teachers for a particular thing or privilege, and is not easily persuaded by their reasoning about alternatives. If Mom or Dad does not give in, they have to prepare themselves for a temper tantrum, destructiveness (e.g., dumping the drawers in the bedroom, kicking a hole in the bedroom wall, or destroying model cars), and verbal abuse ("You don't love me!"; "You are always picking on me!"; "You let Bob [his brother] get away with everything!"). Further, the child may become aggressive toward a brother or sister.

The inability of children to handle frustration and delay generally leads them to become demanding. When they are told something that does not allow them to have their way, they escalate a confrontation which sometimes results in minor war. The difficulty these children have in handling frustration in fact can be viewed as a cause of their demanding nature and aggression.

As a demanding child enters late childhood and adolescence and his/her demands are not being realized, the demands may become manifested in petty thievery and truancy from school. In brief, if their parents do not give in to their material desires, they may simply steal the desired items from the store. If the student does not wish to go to school but instead stays home or runs around with friends, he or she simply may not go to school at all, or may leave the school after signing in.

Impulsive. Impulsivity is seen in a child's acting quickly without forethought and without a consideration of the consequences. Thus, the impulsive child is one who acts as if operating on a dare or a bet. He or she is the child who will be first to try stunts on a bicycle, jump off high places, and act in spite of danger (e.g., lighting a firecracker, shooting a BB gun recklessly, wantonly mixing chemicals from a child's chemical set, using parents' power tools without permission). As you might expect from the above examples, such children have more accidents and broken bones than the average child.

We see impulsivity in young children with aggression and hyperactivity when they enter the first few grades of elementary school. Impulsivity is evident when the child does not print or write legibly because of a failure of his or her thoughts to control the movement of the pen or pencil. Even when a teacher helps the child write and lightly holds his or her hand, the child cannot readily stop the pencil within the boundaries of the paper. In general, the child has difficulty with fine motor control (as exemplified by problems in using scissors, crayons, pens, and pencils). Teachers often describe such children's work as sloppy and careless.

Planning ahead and delaying short-term gains for long-term rewards are very uncharacteristic of the child with conduct problems. Consequently, it is difficult to persuade the impulsive child to prepare for piano lessons, study for school quizzes, or even practice physical prowess activities (e.g., drill with a basketball or soccer ball). Initiative is difficult to encourage when perseverance is necessary to complete a task.

Academic Deficiency and Learning Disabilities. Between 50 and 75 percent of children with aggression and hyperactivity are at least one year behind their peers academically. They are often described by their teachers as underachievers. This finding should not come as a surprise because children with attentional and motivational difficulties may often be unable to sustain performance at academic tasks as long as their peers. However, children with problems of aggression and hyperactivity are not generally mentally retarded. Such children have specific areas of difficulty, but these specific problem areas may result from perceptual, auditory, or verbal deficits, not from intellectual or mental retardation.

Children with hyperactivity and aggression often have learning disabilities. A learning disability refers to a learning problem of children with normal intelligence in the absence of any apparent physical, intellectual, or emotional defect that can be seen as causing the problem. As such, "learning disability" is a purely descriptive term referring to a problem without a known cause. It refers to a discrepancy between expected academic performance and actual achievement. The meaning of the term "learning disability" is important for several reasons:

1. It places the responsibility for helping children with learning problems squarely in the hands of educators rather than placing the responsibility with medicine and drugs (Ross, 1976).

2. Because the term is fairly well accepted by professionals and legislators, it is often the key term which allows a child to have access to special educational, psychological, or medical services.

The term "learning disability" is used to cover a multitude of problems, and until various subcategories of learning disability are delineated, the term will be misused. Further, given the rudimentary state of knowledge in this field, a learning disability merely states that a child has unusual difficulty in learning. Some research initially suggested that the inability to learn resulted from a central problem of selective attention, meaning that the child attends to one aspect of a stimulus to the exclusion of other parts of the stimulus (Ross, 1976). Others view the central problem in learning disability to be motivational; that is, the child does not choose to work because he or she does not find it rewarding. It is important for our purposes here to note that severe learning problems can lead children to become disruptive in the classroom and to develop strong conduct problems. When there is any suspicion of serious academic difficulty, parents should be alert to the need for sound educational evaluation before they spend years of time and effort in psychological therapies. The suspicion should be especially important when a child has one area in which he or she experiences considerable difficulty and at the same time he or she performs at grade level in other subjects.

Children with problems of aggression and hyperactivity frustrate teachers because the teachers know that the children are intellectually normal, at least as defined by an intelligence test, but the children's academic performance often does not reflect their intellectual capability. On the other hand, teachers also perceive these children as challenges to their ability because the children often do have a history of responding well to at least some adult (e.g., Sunday School teacher, grandfather, drum teacher, or gymnastics instructor). Parents and teachers alike in their frustration may resort to epithets, such as "You're lazy!"; "You could do much better!"; "You never work up to your potential." Such remarks may cause the child to withdraw in class, decreasing his or her motivation even further and making him or her even less interested in school work and more apt to look for satisfaction by fooling around. Classroom disruption is the order of the day for these children, and criticism from teachers is very commonplace. In fact, several studies of children with various conduct problems such as hyperactivity and aggression found that about 80 percent of teachers' comments directed to these children were negative!

Hyperactivity. Hyperactivity or hyperkinesis is a term that has been used to describe children with problems of overactivity, inattention, and fidgetiness. It is a term that has been used very widely by professionals and in the public press. The term hyperactive or hyperkinetic has been used to describe a syndrome or set of behaviors that go together, not just to describe a high activity level.

The term hyperactive or hyperkinetic also came to have meaning about the development of the problem. In brief, children who were hyperactive were seen as having Minimal Brain Dysfunction or MBD. The minimal brain dysfunction unfortunately became synonymous with hyperactivity, despite the fact that recent evidence indicates that most children with hyperactivity do not have any brain dysfunction. Fortunately, the term MBD is now being used much less frequently by professionals, and we should be able to return to a more concrete descriptive label, such as hyperactive, which does not infer any particular cause of the behavior.

An essential feature of children with hyperactivity is a persistent pattern of excessive activity, according to Safer and Allen (1976). The pattern of activity occurs year after year, and the child is more active than almost all his peers. Some high activity levels are apparent at one to two years of age, but most activity level problems occur when a child begins school. When a child begins school certain demands occur which require low rates of activity (e.g., listening to a story, resting after snack time, and completing assignments). In fact, differences between children with high and low activity levels are often only apparent during structured lesson times at school, not during free play or unstructured activities.

Impact of Children's Problems on Parents

Marital Discord. Now that you have received a detailed picture of children with conduct disorders, let us look at their effects on parents. In my own clinical practice, I have seen the devastating impact that children with conduct problems can have on parents. While marital discord is a factor in creating and exacerbating problems of children, it is also the case that children who fight a lot and who disobey their parents' wishes often cause important conflict between parents. Unfortunately, one parent often is swept into the role of the defender of the child and the other becomes the prosecutor. In this regard, it is interesting to note that disagreement about child management is one of the most frequently cited reasons for marital discord.

An example from my own clinical practice will illustrate the impact of a boy with conduct disorders on a marriage:

Mrs. Smith initially brought her ten-year-old son, Jim, to see me because of his refusal to complete work at school, his fighting both at home and at school, his unwillingness to stop an activity when his mother or father said "No," his difficulty in communicating with his parents, and his frequent epithets (e.g., "You're a f . . . asshole.") Intelligence tests indicated that he scored within the bright–normal range of intelligence.

After seeing Jim and his parents for six weeks, it became

apparent that Mr. Smith was so disturbed by Jim's actions that he wanted to talk with me about placing Jim with a relative or in a short-term intensive care facility for children. Mr. Smith drank incessantly at parties, and he often drank at home to quell his anger toward Jim. Mrs. Smith's blood pressure was often abnormally high when Jim was causing problems and swearing at her. Mrs. Smith felt that she had to defend Jim when his father wanted to throw him out, causing many arguments and hurt feelings between her and her husband.

This family's situation necessitated a major effort on my part across one and a half years regarding Mr. Smith's alcoholic pattern, Jim's conduct problems, and Mrs. Smith's anxiety and tension level. For our purposes, it is important to note that I addressed the severe negative impact that Jim was having on his parents as well as the ways in which he could make his family life better. Jim and I talked at some length about the necessity for either him or his mother to leave their home for a while because of her blood pressure and anxiety about him. I tried as openly and honestly as possible to convey to Jim that he could prevent a temporary family dissolution by controlling his temper and cooperating both at home and at school. Fortunately, Mr. Smith stopped drinking altogether, Mrs. Smith's blood pressure decreased, and Jim improved markedly. His problem, however, was so severe initially that he will undoubtedly have anger outbursts in the future, but he realizes the clear impact, both positive and negative, that he has on his parents' marriage and his family's general happiness.

Guilt. Mothers are especially prone to guilt feelings about their child with conduct problems. They report concerns about too little time spent with their child and guilt about working when the child was young. Single women report guilt over divorcing their husbands and having to deal with their child's feeling of loss of his or her father. Nor are fathers exempt from this guilt; while they seldom express their guilt, they often reveal that they feel caught in a bind of trying to please themselves and their wives by working at two jobs, meeting financial obligations, and at the same time wanting to see their children. Unfortunately, the children often take a backseat to financial obligations. Even more unfortunately, these financial obligations are self-imposed and relate to materialistic orientations (e.g., a bigger house, a second car), not the necessities of life. This problem of guilt is not limited to couples with financial problems—self-imposed or not. Professionals and business persons with large salaries, especially men, often see their children infrequently, if at all, during the week. Children often have a sense of loss of their parents, and they verbalize their sadness, resentment, and anger with comments such as:

"You're never home! You never have time to play with me. Jimmy's dad next door throws a baseball with him every day after he comes home from work."

"Mom, I expected you to be home by 3:30 when I got home from school. Most mothers of kids in my class [third grade] give their kids a snack and talk with them when they come home from school. You are late so often that I'm going to start going to my friend's house after school!"

"Dad, you make so much money now that I can't see why you don't get a partner to cover for your practice. Other doctors have people who cover for them so that they don't have to have a beeper in their pocket all the time and so they can plan some family activities. We can never plan on anything that involves you. . . . You just answer, 'Delivering babies is not under my control!' "

Parents use such comments from their children to manipulate their spouses, and they attempt to induce further guilt by their own comments. For example, we hear:

"The exact time a mother begins labor is not under your control, but you do have control over whether or not you hire someone to cover for you on weekends or on your so-called day off."

"If you'd just talk to the kids for a while when you get home rather than withdraw into the den with the newspaper, I wouldn't get so angry."

Summary

Problems of aggression, hyperactivity, inattention, impulsivity, and overactivity are the most frequent problems of children, and they are not simply problems that disappear with maturity. These problems of children are predictive of attendance at mental health clinics as adults. Many children with hyperactivity and aggression also have academic problems and learning disabilities. While we know that children's problems are often a result of parental practices, it is also becoming clear that children with various behavioral problems can have a deleterious effect on a marriage. Finally, the guilt experienced by parents—especially mothers—of such children who feel they have failed with their children is often tremendous. My purpose in the rest of this book will be to help parents and professionals realize that *many* factors of a social and physiological nature lead to aggression and hyperactivity. In addition, I hope to illustrate how such children can progress successfully with the aid of parents and professionals.

References

American Psychiatric Association. *Diagnostic and Statistical Manual III*. Washington, DC: Author, 1980.

Churchill, W. *My early life: A roving commission*. New York: Charles Schribner, 1930.

Olweus, D. *Aggression in the schools: Bullies and Whipping Boys*. New York: Halstead Press, Wiley, 1978.

Quay, H. C. Classification. In H. C. Quay & J. S. Werry (Eds.), *Psychopathological disorders of childhood* (2nd Ed.). New York: John Wiley and Sons, 1979, 1–42.

Ross. A. O. *Psychological aspects of learning disabilities and reading disorders*. New York: McGraw-Hill, 1976.

Schrag, P., & Divoky, D. *The myth of the hyperactive child*. New York: Pantheon, 1975

World Health Organization. *Manual of the international statistical classification of diseases, injuries, and causes of death*. Ninth Revision, 1977. Geneva, Switzerland: Author, 1977.

2

Frequency, Diagnosis, and Prognosis

Frequency

The estimated percentage of children with behavioral problems varies somewhat from country to country, but most teachers will conclude that two children in an average size classroom of 25–30 children have such marked problems with aggression, impulsivity, and overactivity that these problems interfere significantly with their learning.

The U.S. Department of Health, Education and Welfare in 1971 stated that approximately 5 percent of children in the United States are hyperactive, and that figure has been generally confirmed by investigators in Australia, China, Germany, South Africa, and New Zealand, using standardized rating scales for teachers. The criterion for defining hyperactivity is a criterion of extremity. That is, if a child receives a score placing him or her in the upper 5 percent of the population on activity level, he or she is defined as hyperactive. These studies indicate that if one adds the children who have problems of aggression who are not hyperactive (5 percent), the percentage of children with behavioral problems of one form or another becomes 10 percent.

Sex differences. In almost all prevalent studies of child behavior problems, males are judged more than three times as often to have the problem as females. These behavioral problems are especially marked by aggression, and aggression is decidedly more predominant in males than females. Aggression is generally thought of as one of the most unequivocal psychological differences between the sexes. Further, apparently this difference cannot be explained away by simply looking at differences in how aggression is expressed (Maccoby & Jacklin, 1974).

29

Reasons for this sex difference are multiple, but socialization and biological differences are the two major explanations for the difference. Differential socialization of males and females has long been an explanation supported by research findings. More specifically, it is thought that both males and females reward aggression more frequently in male children than in female. Interestingly, even in societies where women are judged to be the more aggressive and dominant, the men fight in wars—not the women (Eme, 1979).

Despite sex differences in aggression that might be attributed to different socialization processes for males and females, experts in developmental psychology are quick to note that different socialization for boys and girls is not the sole explanation for such differences. For example, Maccoby and Jacklin (1974) contended that biological differences between males and females account for the observed differences in aggression. It has been shown that injections of male hormones into female animals will make the females more aggressive and more active than if they had not had the injection. While these animal models must be used with caution in extrapolating to human conditions, the evidence from varying areas points to certain hormonal differences in males and females that may account for differences in activity level and aggression.

Diagnosis

Rating scales. In order to assess whether your child or a child you are seeing professionally can be judged as having a serious problem, you may wish to complete the checklist below or give it to the child's parents or teacher to complete. If a child's parent or teacher checks 12 or more of the 16 items on this checklist, he or she then has a score comparable to that of children who are taken by their parents to psychological clinics for therapy. Based on the responses of hundreds of parents of clinic and non-clinic children, only 5 percent of all children receive a score of 12 or greater.

Peterson-Quay Behavior Problem Checklist

(University of Illinois, 1967)

Instructions: Please indicate which of the following constitute problems, as far as the child is concerned. If the item does *not* constitute a problem, check ''No''; if the item constitutes a mild or severe problem, check ''Yes.''

Item   Yes   No

1 ——— ——— Attention-seeking, ''show off'' behavior.
2 ——— ——— Restlessness, inability to sit still.
3 ——— ——— Disruptiveness, tendency to bother others.

4 ——— ——— Dislike for school.
5 ——— ——— Jealousy over attention paid to other children.
6 ——— ——— Fighting.
7 ——— ——— Temper tantrums.
8 ——— ——— Irresponsibility, undependability.
9 ——— ——— Disobedience, difficulty in disciplinary control.
10 ——— ——— Uncooperativeness in group situations.
11 ——— ——— Hyperactivity, always on the go.
12 ——— ——— Destructiveness in regard to his or her own or others' property.
13 ——— ——— Impertinence, sauciness.
14 ——— ——— Profane language.
15 ——— ——— Irritability, hot tempered, easily aroused to anger.
16 ——— ——— Negativism, tendency to do the opposite of what is requested of him or her.

Total ———

The teacher of a child whose behavior may seem problematic may be able to provide you with very useful information by completing the abbreviated checklist below (Abbreviated Conners Teacher Rating Scale). If the child receives a score of 20 or greater on this scale, he or she will fall within the top 5 percent of the elementary school population on this assessment device. The cutoff score of 20 is applicable in the U.S., Australia, South Africa, New Zealand, Germany, and probably other Western European countries.

The previous scale as well as the one below have been used extensively throughout the world. It is often advisable to have ratings from both parents and teachers before reaching any firm conclusion about how a child is perceived. Furthermore, if a child has two teachers, it is advisable to ask both teachers to complete the form. Caution must be used in interpreting the results of these scales without seeking professional help. *These are fallible instruments*, as are all assessment devices, but they have proven most useful for preliminary screening.

Abbreviated Conners' Teacher Rating Scale

Instructions: Please indicate which of the following constitute problems, as far as the child is concerned.

Observation		Degree of Activity			
		Not At All	Just a Little	Pretty Much	Very Much
CLASSROOM BEHAVIOR	Score	0	1	2	3
Constantly fidgeting					
Demands must be met immediately— easily frustrated					
Restless or overactive					
Excitable, impulsive					
Inattentive, easily distracted					
Fails to finish things he/she starts—short attention span					

Cries often and easily

Disturbs other children

Mood changes quickly and
   drastically

Temper outbursts, explosive and
   unpredictable behavior

        Sum

                             Grand Sum

Child   Date   Teacher

Psychological tests. The most frequently used tests with children suspected of problems of aggression and hyperactivity are intelligence tests (Wechsler Intelligence Scale for Children and Stanford Binet Intelligence Test) and tests of visual motor impairment (e.g., Bender-Gestalt). Intelligence tests are given to assess whether a child is behind in school because he or she lacks the intelligence to perform as well as others. Usually parents are correct in thinking that their child is at least of average intelligence, but, on occasion, a child may be behind because he/she does not have the general intellectual skills of others his/her age.

Intelligence tests have their greatest use in predicting how well a child will do in school. In fact, IQ tests that are individually administered are the best predictors of school achievement known. IQ tests administered by teachers or guidance counselors are not as reliable as individually administered tests, and they are often misused by teachers. For example, it is not uncommon for a young child to be anxious when he or she takes a group IQ test for the first time. This anxiety can lead a child to do poorly, and sometimes a teacher will categorize a child as having average or below average intelligence when in fact the child scored poorly simply because he or she was anxious. If the child were given an individually administered IQ test by a psychologist, it is the psychologist's job to put the child at ease and to do everything possible to alleviate the child's anxiety before a test is administered.

Other factors can also lead to low IQ scores which may result in misinterpretation and misapplication of IQ tests. Children who have English as their second language have been known to be erroneously placed in classes for mentally retarded. In California, this problem became so critical that children can no longer be placed in classes for the mentally retarded on the basis of group administered tests. Such placements must be based on a professional's interpretation of intelligence test scores after considering language barriers, ethnic background and emotional problems. Children with emotional problems such as unusual sensitivity to criticism, poor attention span, and high rates of motor activity certainly may not do well on intelligence tests administered in a group situation. Any time you believe that your child has greater capability than indicated by the school or some professional outside the school, you should receive a second opinion by a private licensed psychologist who is not allied with the particular school in question.

While there are problems with the interpretation and use of intelligence tests, they can be very helpful when handled by an experienced psychologist. In addition to their use in predicting performance in school, a psychologist can obtain leads about other factors to be assessed by watching a child perform in the highly standardized format of an intelligence test. The psychologist will assess how well a child does on various subtests of an IQ test, and the psychologist will be able to make judgments about whether other tests to assess visual motor ability, memory, ability to understand information given verbally or in written form or verbal expressiveness are appropriate.

The Bender-Gestalt Test involves having the child reproduce a series of geometric designs or forms, and it is used to assess visual-motor impairment and minimal brain injury, both of which are associated with below average reading and writing performance.

The Bender-Gestalt Test is often used as a screening device by psychologists who are concerned about whether there is some neurological damage or dysfunction. If a child does poorly on the Bender-Gestalt Test, a referral may be made to a neurologist for a more complete examination. Such a referral is most likely if there have been some seizures or there has been a recent and dramatic change in a child's functioning.

Clinical interview. You may now feel that your child or a child you know well has many of the symptoms described in this book. The next logical question you may raise is: Would a psychologist or psychiatrist feel that my child needs treatment? To ascertain whether a child needs treatment and to determine possible causes for current problems, a mental health practitioner would probably interview the child, the parents, and perhaps the teacher.

An experienced clinician will seek information regarding several areas during the course of interviews with the parents and child:

1. Infancy: Were there pregnancy or birth difficulties?

2. Preschool Years: Were there any unusual medical complications during early childhood? Were there difficulties in sleeping, eating, and motor restlessness? Did the child have great difficulty accepting "no" for an answer? Did the child have opportunities to play with others to learn social skills (e.g., were there kids his or her age in the neighborhood; did the child go to nursery school)?

3. School Years: Did the child have difficulty learning to accept the school routine in first grade? Did the child have visual problems (e.g., reversals of letters, focusing problem)? Is there one subject which presents special problems for the child? Are there social problems both at home and at school? Are there serious marital problems? How does the child view him/herself?

After a careful integration of data from the rating scales, psychological tests, and clinical interviews with child, parents, and teachers, a specific diagnosis can be made.

Why is there a Diagnosis?

If your child has problems of aggression, hyperactivity, and impulsivity, and if you go to a psychologist or psychiatrist for an assessment of your child, the child may receive an official diagnosis of "Conduct Disorder" or "Attention Deficit Disorder with Hyperactivity." The child need not know about the diagnosis, and often the diagnosis may not even be discussed with the parent. The diagnosis is simply noted in the child's record.

Many parents ask, "Why are diagnostic labels used at all?" Psychologists and psychiatrists who work in county, state, and federal facilities are required to provide diagnoses of all children they see or to state that no problem was observed. The diagnoses are required because government officials need estimates of the types of problems that occur within their regions in order to plan effectively for providing service to various groups of children. To receive reimbursement from insurance companies, a diagnosis is needed from a mental health professional.

In order to develop treatment for any problems, there has to be a method for classifying the problems. The diagnostic system is the method of classifying problems of a psychological or psychiatric nature. The classification or diagnostic system allows researchers to find out whether certain types of treatments work for certain types of individuals. Without a diagnostic or classification system, progress in treating diseases and psychological problems would be impossible.

Communication among professionals is aided by diagnostic systems. When a doctor in one state sends records of a patient to a doctor in another state when the patient moves, use of a diagnosis, some supporting comments about the diagnosis, and a detailed care record will facilitate communication between the two doctors. The communication is facilitated because the doctors understand that if a child has a certain diagnosis (e.g., "Attention Deficit with Hyperactivity") certain factors about the child must be addressed that might not be addressed if the child had a different diagnosis (e.g., there may be some neurological problems; medication or alteration in diet may be necessary).

Some parents worry about a diagnosis being placed on any records of a child such as an insurance form or a physician's or psychologist's records. These records are confidential, and in the United States information from a professional, an insurance company, or a mental health facility cannot be released to anyone without parent approval.

Prognosis

In a classic study by Lee Robbins, it was found that children with a variety of conduct problems who had attended a general mental health clinic were the children most likely to have problems as adults. As Dr. Robbins stated in 1979, "Serious antisocial behavior . . . presages [predicts] lifelong problems with the law, inability to earn a living, defective interpersonal relationships, and severe personal stress. In fact, if one could successfully treat the antisocial behavior of childhood, the problems of adult crime, alcoholism, divorce, and chronic unemployment might be significantly diminished." (p. 509)

If you have a child or relative with serious problems of aggression, impulsivity, and overactivity, you may wonder about how *likely* it is that such children will have significant problems as adults. The Robbins study will be described briefly to indicate the types of children followed in this long-range study. Robbins studied 524 children referred to a child guidance clinic in the U.S. between 1924 and 1929. The preponderance of the children (approximately 75 percent) were referred to the clinic for varied antisocial behavior; further, approximately 50 percent of the children had had contact with the juvenile court.

A comparison group of 100 children matched with the clinic children for age, sex, IQ, and socioeconomic status was also obtained from school records. These children also attended school between 1924 and 1929 and were interviewed 30 years after the 1924–1929 period. Detailed social, medical, and psychiatric histories were obtained as well as court, hospital, and employment records.

The most important finding was that antecedents of antisocial behavior in adulthood were evident in the children's records. The greater the severity and frequency of antisocial behavior of the child, the more likely that the child would later be diagnosed as sociopathic as an adult (having antisocial or sexually deviant behavior).

The children in the Robbins study had more serious and frequent antisocial behavior than the average child referred to a child mental health clinic today. Thus, you should not conclude that your child will grow up to have serious problems as an adult if he or she simply has problems of handling frustration, over-activity, and aggression. That prediction should only seem plausible if the child in question has severe conduct problems *and* if the child has had legal infractions.

In a study executed in England by Shepard and colleagues in the early 1960s, 50 children who attended a mental health clinic were compared with 50 children who were similar in age and sex to the clinic sample, but who had not attended a mental health clinic. Children in the clinic samples who were psychotic and severely antisocial and who had contact with the court were excluded from the comparison. Two years following the initial contact, an interview was conducted and there were few differences obtained between the clinic and nonclinic children. While the Shepard study did not contain information on the frequency and type of treatment the children received, it did seem apparent that, with the children having severe antisocial behavior excluded, the other children appeared to progress remarkably well.

We have been discussing long-term evaluations of children labeled aggressive. We will now turn to a description of long-term evaluations with hyperactive children. Comparisons were made between adolescents who had been diagnosed as hyperactive as children but who were not treated and adolescents who: (1) were matched on age, sex, social class, and IQ; (2) had never failed a grade; and (3) had had neither parent complain that they were or had been a behavior problem. The formerly diagnosed hyperactive children when assessed in young adulthood had made more geographic moves and had had more car and motorcycle accidents. The formerly diagnosed hyperactive children had completed fewer years of education than the comparison children, and as might be expected, they also had received poorer marks in school and had been expelled from school more than the comparison children. Psychiatric interview evaluations indicated that the formerly diagnosed hyperactive children had fewer friends, felt more restless in the interview, and were more likely to be described by the psychiatrists as impulsive and immature-dependent than comparison children.

Of extreme interest were the reactions of the formerly diagnosed hyperactive children to the question, "What helped you most during childhood?" The most common response was, "A mother who believed in my potential for success," "A teacher who recognized my worth," or "My discovery of a particular talent I had." If you are a parent of a child with conduct problems or if you counsel parents of children similar to those described in this book, the reactions of the formerly diagnosed hyperactive kids to things that made their childhood better or worse should receive special attention. Of greatest negative impact were: "Family fights about me," "Feeling inferior and dumb," and "Being criticized." Significantly more hyperactive children rated their childhood as unhappy than did the comparison children.

As noted earlier, the diagnosis of hyperactivity can be differentiated reliably from the diagnosis of conduct disorder. However, a number of children receive a primary diagnosis of hyperactivity (Attention Deficit Disorder with Hyperactivity), and a secondary diagnosis of Conduct Disorder. Others receive a primary diagnosis of Conduct Disorder and a secondary diagnosis of Attention Deficit Disorder. Information about the degree of aggression in children is a useful predictor of later adjustment. Loney and her collegues (Langhorne & Loney, 1979) followed 135 children who were labeled hyperactive, but she separated the children into two groups based on the children's levels of aggression. She found that the children in the higher level of aggression group had more adjustment problems as adolescents and were *less* responsive to medication for hyperactivity than the other group.

It can be concluded that if a child has serious aggression problems, the child is at risk for many later problems of adjustment. From studies of children referred to courts to studies of children without court involvement but who have been referred to mental health or pediatric clinics, it is clear that the greater the child's level of aggression, the greater will be his or her socialization problems.

However, a less obvious problem of children with problems of hyperactivity and aggression is their difficulty in academic areas. If a child is impulsive and has difficulty attending, his or her achievement will be markedly affected. For example, if a ten-year-old child with hyperactivity and aggression is behind two years in reading and/or math, without special aid the child's achievement decrement will simply widen across time. That is, he/she will fall farther and farther behind his/her peers in academic subjects, in turn creating problems of low self-esteem. The academic problems of children are too often not well attended to by mental health personnel who are primarily concerned with the social well-being of the child. In fact, however, without addressing the child's academic problems, it is nearly impossible for the child to really feel that he or she has progressed markedly.

A child in elementary school derives his or her self-esteem to a large degree from academic achievement, and the repeated academic failure of children with hyperactivity and aggression must be addressed. When a child cannot receive attention through socially defined appropriate channels, he or she will readily gravitate toward misbehavior. Misbehavior, such as clowning in a classroom, usually results in both teacher and peer attention. While the teacher attention may be negative, the peer laughter and even encouragement of more clowning will often be enough to prompt the child to seek a role that becomes rewarding enough to offset many frustrations of academic deficiency. Other children with various conduct disorders and academic deficiency who are not as extroverted as the clown may simply daydream in class and withdraw from the academic scene. Occasionally, their frustration with their own academic deficiency may lead to aggressive outbursts on the playground or even in the classroom itself. In sum, the academic deficiencies of children with problems of aggression and hyperactivity must be addressed, or the positive prognosis of the children will be clearly hampered.

Summary

Approximately 10 percent of elementary school children throughout the world have problems of hyperactivity, aggression, and impulse control. About 5 percent of elementary school children in the United States are seen as hyperactive, and about 5 percent of the children are seen as having conduct disorders. Boys are about three times as likely to have these problems of aggression and hyperactivity as girls.

To assess whether a child has serious problems of hyperactivity and aggression, rating schedules for parents and teachers have been standardized in many countries throughout the world. Psychological tests such as intelligence tests (Wechsler Intelligence Test for Children and the Stanford Binet Intelligence Test) and tests of psychomotor difficulty (Bender-Gestalt Test) are used to determine intellectual level, visual-motor problems, and possible neurological deficit. Clinical interviews are also used with children and their parents to determine birth, developmental, and family status.

Problems of hyperactivity and aggression are predictive of difficulties in adolescence and adulthood such as low self-esteem, poor social skills, car and motorcycle accidents, and poor school grades. Of great importance to hyperactive and aggressive children are parents and teachers who believe in them and recognize their worth.

Hyperactivity is a problem that many children and parents learn to cope with even though the activity level of the person may not become "normal" or average after therapy. As we shall see later, many children are helped markedly by various treatments, but many remain quite active throughout life. In such cases, the issue is learning to channel energies or activity level in a positive manner. Inappropriate aggression is a social behavior which can be reduced, and fortunately it can be gradually eliminated in the majority of children.

References

Conners, C. K. A teacher rating scale for use in drug studies with children. *American Journal of Psychiatry*, 1969, *126*, 884–888.

Department of Health, Education and Welfare. Office of Child Development. *Report of the Conference on the use of stimulant drugs in the treatment of behaviorally disturbed young school children.* Washington, D.C.: U.S. Government Printing Office, January, 1971.

Eme, R. F. Sex differences in childhood psychopathology: A Review. *Psychological Bulletin*, 1979, *86*, 574–595.

Maccoby, E., & Jacklin, C. *The psychology of sex differences.* Stanford, CA: Stanford University Press, 1974.

Quay, H. C. Measuring dimensions of deviant behavior: The Behavior Problem Checklist. *Journal of Abnormal Child Psychology*, 1977, *5*, 277–287.

Robbins, L. N. Follow-up studies. In H. C. Quay & J. S. Werry (Eds.), *Psychopathological disorders of childhood* (2nd Ed.). New York: John Wiley and Sons, 1979, 483–513.

Shepard, M., Oppenheim, B., & Mitchell, S. Childhood behavior disorders and the child guidance clinic: An epidemiological study. *Journal of Child Psychology and Psychiatry*, 1966, *7*, 39–52.

Trites, R., Dugas, E., Lynch, G., & Ferguson, H. B. Prevalence of hyperactivity. *Journal of Pediatric Psychology*, 1979, *4*, 179–188.

Weiss, G., Hechtman, L., Perlman, T., Hopkins, J., & Wener, A. Hyperactives as young adults. *Archives of General Psychiatry*, 1979, *36*, 675–681.

3

Biological and Physiological Causes of Aggression and Hyperactivity

Active, impulsive, and aggressive behavior does not have a single cause, and in some cases, biological factors may contribute to such behavior. For example, studies involving adopted children and twins indicate that an individual's heredity may strongly influence his or her activity level. Many people believe that certain chromosomal abnormalities predispose an individual to impulsive and aggressive behavior. Furthermore, it appears that levels of particular hormones in one's body may influence the degree of aggressive behavior exhibited by an individual. Finally, current research indicates that a tendency towards aggressive and hyperactive behavior is associated with a physiological sensitivity to certain substances such as sugar, artificial food dyes, or lead. In this chapter, we will examine these various biological causes of aggression and hyperactivity.

Heredity

It has long been felt that we inherit predispositions to be active, impulsive, and aggressive. It is commonly noted that aggression and hyperactivity are traits of several members of a particular family. When talking to parents of hyperactive or aggressive children, I often hear the parents report that they had the same problem when they were young and that they feel that their son or daughter inherited a family trait. Similarly, many animal lovers know that certain dogs (e.g., Irish setters and fox terriers) are very active while others may be more passive and calm (e.g., collies). Furthermore, even within the same breed, dogs can be selectively mated to produce certain temperaments.

Although there are no studies which directly link aggression

43

and genetic factors in humans, there is considerable evidence to
suggest that an individual's characteristic level of activity may
be inherited. The basic evidence for a genetic component in
activity level comes from two sources: adoption studies and twin
studies.

Adoption studies. Adoption studies are often difficult to interpret
because many children are not adopted immediately at birth, but
at some later time. The longer the time the child is reared by his
or her natural parents, the more difficult it is to determine the
extent to which similarities between a child and his or her parents
are due to heredity, and which are due to learning from the
parents. At any rate, comparisons of the natural parents and
adoptive parents of adopted hyperactive children show that more
natural parents were hyperactive themselves as children than
were adoptive parents.

Twin studies. Reports of mothers of same-sex twins indicate that
activity level is much more alike for monozygotic (same egg)
twins than for dizygotic (different egg) twins (Willerman, 1973).
In addition, the relationship between activity level and attention
span is more similar for monozygotic twins than for dizygotic
twins (Fuller and Thompson, 1978). Because the genetic material
of monozygotic twins is identical, these findings lend support
to the role of heredity in influencing activity level. It is important
to bear in mind that even though a personality trait may be
heritable, it still may be changeable. In fact, activity level is one
trait which appears to be influenced by genetic factors but is also
quite changeable across time.

Chromosomal Abnormality

Normal males have an XY pair of chromosomes, and females
have an XX pair. As you might expect, the Y chromosome
determines whether an individual is a male or a female. However,
in approximately one or two instances in 1,000 males, there is
an extra Y chromosome that results from double fertilization of
the ovum. Because one Y chromosome causes an individual to
be male, it was thought by some that two Y chromosomes would

create a "supermale," that is, a male with exaggerated masculine characteristics. Indeed, surveys have shown that XYY men are, on the average, six inches taller than normal men. In addition, surveys of imprisoned criminals indicate that among criminal populations, there is a greater percentage of men with XYY than exists in the general population.

The XYY chromosome syndrome was used as evidence in the defense of Daniel Hugon in a murder trial in Paris in 1968. Hugon's attorneys argued that his chromosome anomaly was the cause of his violent behavior. While he was convicted of murder, he did receive a diminished sentence in part because of the chromosomal anomaly. The XYY syndrome also gained visibility in the highly publicized mass murder case of Richard Speck, who senselessly killed eight nurses in Chicago, Illinois, in 1968. During an appeal of Speck's murder conviction, there was an air of uncertainty about his likely sentence because he purportedly had the XYY chromosomal makeup. However, it was later learned that Speck's chromosome structure was normal, and Speck's murder conviction was retained.

One of the largest studies of the XYY condition was conducted in France by Noel and colleagues in 1974. 15,000 young men undergoing compulsory medical checkups were examined. Only 20 XYY men were found, and none of them had criminal records. In another study of the XYY syndrome, the subjects were 4,139 Danish men who were taller than average. Chromosomal analysis revealed 12 XYY's; five of the XYY men (42 percent) had a record of some sort of criminal conviction, whereas only 9 percent of the general population of Danish men have criminal convictions (Witkin, et al., 1976).

In summary, the only unanimous result from studies of the XYY syndrome is that such males are taller than average. Secondly, there is only suggestive evidence of an association between XYY and aggression or violence, and this evidence comes from a very small number of males who were screened from large populations in France and Denmark.

Since the likelihood of having an XYY abnormality is so

extremely low in the general population, it is not very useful to resort to chromosomal abnormalities as causes for aggression. Even among criminal population, the prevalence of the XYY abnormality is only 2 percent (Jarvik, Klodin, and Matsuyma, 1973)! In brief, even if there were a direct association between the XYY condition and aggression or violence, the condition would account for a very small amount of the violence in our society. The search for a chromosomal abnormality as the cause of aggression and violence may be partly understood because we often find it difficult to attribute heinous crimes such as mass murders to social and family causes. However, as we shall see later in this book, the social and family causes of aggression seem gigantic when compared to chromosomal abnormalities.

Hormones

It is well known that adolescent boys become more aggressive as they approach puberty. In addition, the levels of the male hormone, testosterone, increase dramatically from ages 10 to 15. Interestingly, however, testosterone levels have not been related to aggression in general populations of adolescents. That is, male adolescents with high testosterone levels are not necessarily more aggressive than those with low testosterone levels. However, with 14- to 19-year-old males selected from juvenile offenders at a correctional institution in Utah, testosterone levels were related to assaultive behavior (Moyer, 1976). Similarly, with general populations of young men aged 17 to 28, testosterone levels were very highly correlated with the young men's descriptions of their own aggressiveness.

Direct manipulation of hormones is not ethically possible with humans, but studies with animals confirm the notion that aggression is influenced by male sex hormones. Administration of testosterone in female hamsters increases their aggression. Similarly, when male hormones are injected into pregnant monkeys, their female offspring will be more aggressive than other female offspring who did not receive such an injection.

Hormone Levels and Aggressiveness of Hockey Players
College hockey players from a nationally ranked eastern team were rated by two team coaches on a seven-item scale to assess aggressiveness. Aggressiveness referred to variables such as body contact, offensiveness, and competitiveness. Blood sample levels of the male hormone testosterone indicated that testosterone was related to body contact, aggressive responses to threats, and global aggressiveness. Aggressive responses to threats were highly and significantly correlated with levels of testosterone.

From Scaramella, T. J. & Brown, W. A. "Serum testosterone and aggressiveness in hockey players." *Psychosomatic Medicine*, 1978, *40*, No. 3, 262–265.

In sum, there is certainly suggestive evidence that testosterone and aggression are related in humans. Further, direct manipulation of testosterone in animals indicates a clear relationship between male hormones and aggression. However, with humans, social learning processes most likely are more important in the expression of aggression than are hormone levels. More importantly, for our purposes here it should be emphasized that while elevated male hormone levels may increase the likelihood of aggression for adults, there have been no demonstrations that aggression in young children is correlated with male hormones.

Brain Dysfunction

In 1902, Dr. Still first reported that hyperactivity appeared to be the result of various brain dysfunctions, such as tumors, head injury, and meningitis (inflammation of the brain and spinal cord). An epidemic of encephalitis, or brain inflammation, in the United States in 1918 led to further confirmation that brain dysfunction can cause hyperactivity. Unfortunately, brain dysfunction became seen as the cause of most cases of hyperactivity. However, since brain dysfunctions were not apparent from the electroencephalograms (EEGs) or neurological examinations of most hyperactive children, it was concluded that some sort of minimal brain dysfunction (MBD) caused hyperactivity.

In 1966, the U.S. Department of Health, Education, and
Welfare published a monograph, "Minimal Brain Dysfunction,"
which dealt with problems of terminology and conceptualization
of childhood problems thought to be a result of brain dysfunction.
Since the publication of that report, minimal brain dysfunction
has received widespread publicity in both scientific and public
arenas. The difficulty with the diagnosis MBD is that researchers
have not conclusively confirmed that there are any differences
in brain dysfunction, minimal or otherwise, between groups of
children diagnosed as hyperactive or MBD and randomly-selected children of the same age and sex. Typically, the diagnosis
of MBD is made on the basis of indirect signs of brain dysfunction, such as problems with fine motor control, rather than
direct evidence of brain dysfunction, such as EEG recordings.
This absence of differences between children diagnosed as MBD
and randomly-selected groups of children in direct signs of brain
dysfunction led some clinicians to abandon the notion of brain
dysfunction as a cause of hyperactivity. However, other clinicians argued that since certain medication causes hyperactive
children to improve markedly in their social behavior and in their
fine motor skills, this improvement supported the notion that
hyperactive children have a brain dysfunction. In 1979, an ex-
periment was conducted which shattered this notion that response
to medication indicates the existence of brain damage. Rapoport
and her colleagues gave the same medication to normal children
that had been shown to help hyperactive children's social behavior and fine motor skills. To many people's amazement,
Rapoport and her colleagues (Rapoport, Buchsbaum, Zahn *et
al.*, 1978) found that normal children showed almost the same
kinds of response to the medication as the hyperactive children
showed. That is, the normal children showed increased memory,
and improved performance on tasks requiring sustained attention
and redirection of activity.

Although brain dysfunctions are certainly not the cause of
most hyperactive and aggressive behavior, between 5 and 10
percent of hyperactive children do have psychological problems

that are associated with brain dysfunction. For example, some hyperactive children have extreme difficulty printing and writing. In addition, some hyperactive children have coordination problems such as difficulty in riding a bicycle or throwing and catching a ball. Thus, if you feel that your child or your patient has unusual difficulty with gross motor coordination, it may be helpful to have him or her checked by a neurologist for brain abnormalities.

Physiological Sensitivity

In an era when there is an emphasis on physical fitness, a strong focus on diet should be expected. In fact, slogans and by-lines in newspapers often relfect the notion "You Are What You Eat." Health food stores which promote foods that do not contain chemical additives and which rely on natural food processing have flourished in many parts of the world. In recent years, the Non-Fiction Best Seller List generally contains at least one book pertaining to diet. In this context, it is easy to see how the view that one's diet causes hyperactivity has caught world-wide attention.

The notion that a relationship exists between diet and hyperactivity was proposed by Dr. Benjamin Feingold. As an allergist (a physician specializing in diagnosis and treatment of problems such as hay fever, asthma, and allergic reactions to foods), he observed that some of his patients seemed to show strong adverse reactions, including agitated behavior, to aspirin and salicylates (chemical compounds similar to aspirin). Because of his suspicions that these patients had an allergic reaction to aspirin and salicylates, Feingold placed them on a diet free of such chemicals. Their responses were reported to be dramatic, with the allergic symptoms and frenetic behavior disappearing within several weeks. Dr. Feingold, however, realized that there was no specific allergy to aspirin that could be detected by blood tests. He then revised his allergic reaction theory to a physiological sensitivity notion. More specifically, he argued that children with this type of physiological sensitivity should be placed on a diet free of natural salicylate compounds that are contained in foods such as apricots, prunes, peaches, plums, raspberries, grapes, oranges, cucumbers, and tomatoes. In addition, he argued that foods containing artificial food coloring and a preservative, BHT, Butolated Hydroxy Tolune, should be removed from everyone's diet. Feingold reported that when he placed hyperactive children on a diet free of salicylate compounds, 30 percent showed a response he termed "dramatic," and 18 percent responded "favorably."

If one looks at *all* of the studies on food coloring and salicylates, the most one can now conclude is that a very small percentage of children may show negative reactions to food coloring or salicylates, and children less than six years old seem to be most likely affected.

Another related dietary concern regarding hyperactivity has been the amount of sugar children eat. The Feingold diet involves elimination of many citrus fruits with sugar, and some researchers thought that some children might react positively to the reduction of sugar in their diet. In fact, Prinz and his co-workers found a very significant relationship between amount of sugar eaten daily and the rates of aggression and restlessness exhibited in the playroom by hyperactive children (Prinz, Roberts & Hartman, 1980). The amount of sugar consumed was estimated from a mother's daily record of food intake for seven days.

Prinz realized that one interpretation of these results could be that parents who allow their children to eat high amounts of sugar may be less careful and consistent in their general discipline, and it may in fact be the inconsistent discipline rather than the sugar intake that was associated with the hyperactive behavior. To address this issue, Prinze and his colleagues measured general parental competence, education level, and socioeconomic status, and found that across all levels of these variables, there still was a highly significant association between sugar ingestion and aggression and restlessness. Thus, this study should certainly lead parents of hyperactive or aggressive children to be cautious regarding the amount of sugar that exists in their children's diets. It is of interest to note, however, that Prinz and his colleagues did not find any association between sugar intake and aggression in children who did not have behavioral problems.

Other scientists (Trites, Tryphonas, and Ferguson, 1980) have confirmed that there is a positive relationship between a teacher's rating of hyperactivity and the number of allergies present in a hyperactive child, especially when the hyperactive children have learning disabilities or a diagnosis of minimal brain dysfunction. In particular, such hyperactive children showed allergic reactions to proteins of plant and animal origin such as oats, certain cereals, pork, beef, chicken, eggs, and soybeans. These allergic reactions were determined by specific antibodies in their blood. As we shall discuss later, however, when a diet that eliminated the foodstuffs thought to be responsible for the hyperactivity was given to the children, they showed no greater improvement than the improvement shown by children who were on some placebo diet (a diet that eliminated certain foodstuffs not thought to be related to hyperactivity).

One explanation of this finding may be that children with behavior problems such as aggression and hyperactivity are simply more metabolically sensitive to many foodstuffs than children without such problems. For example, it may be the case that hyperactive children have a greater tendency to be allergic to artificial food dyes (Swanson and Kinsbourne, 1980), animal and plant proteins (Trites, et al., 1980), and to sugar (Prinz, et al., 1980). It does not follow from such research, however, that elimination or reduction of dye, animal and plant protein, and sugar will necessarily lead to a reduction in hyperactivity or aggression. As a clinician who works daily with problems of aggression and hyperactivity in children, I advise you as parents to observe carefully your child in case he or she does show adverse reactions to certain foodstuffs, and to see if elimination of such foodstuffs could lead to a reduction of behavior problems *in your child.*

Lead

Children who live in old, dilapidated buildings where they can eat paint chips that fall from ceilings or walls are in danger of lead poisoning. Infants can also eat paint with a lead base from windowsills and furniture. When children eat paint chips that have a lead base, they can suffer serious neurological problems such as severe hyperactivity due to lead poisoning in the blood. Such damage occurs only when there is repeated ingestion of small amounts of lead over several months, but this is not uncommon in large cities where housing conditions are poor. Fortunately, paints with a lead base are produced much less frequently than they used to be, and when lead is used in paint, it is often noted on the labels. In addition, some towns in the United States have required lead-painted buildings to be stripped and repainted if children live there (Walker, 1977). Finally, some clinics have free medical diagnostic tests to assess whether children have high amounts of lead in their systems, and there is a method of treating children with a chelating agent (a chemical compound) to reduce their lead levels.

A recent study of Needleman and his colleagues (1979) assessed a very large group of children from two New England towns for lead intake. The baby teeth of these children were collected, and the teeth were then analyzed chemically for lead content. The levels of lead were found to be related to the children's level of disruptive behavior, such as aggression, and attention span in school. Children with the highest lead levels had a greater history of eating non-food objects (pica), which may have included paint that contained lead. Although the investigators did not report the living areas of these children, other recent research indicates that we can get significant amounts of lead in our bodies by inhaling gases and fumes that contain lead. Thus, it would be interesting to record the proximity of these children's residences to areas with high concentrations of lead fumes. In fact, in another study, Needleman and his associates found that children in Philadelphia with high lead levels had lived in areas with many smelters, foundries, and lead-processing plants.

Practical suggestions from the research on the detrimental effects of lead involve different forms of environmental change. Most importantly, industrial pollution from smelters should be closely monitored; lead in paint should be kept very low; and lead pipes for domestic water use should be gradually eliminated. Interestingly, these steps have been more actively pursued in England than in the United States (Rutter, 1980). Efforts are currently in progress in the United States by parent groups and environmental protection groups to reduce lead in our environment. Lead in gasoline allows greater mileage per gallon and allows engines to run at cooler temperatures. Given the frequent shortages of gasoline due to intermittent world conflicts and restriction of sales by Mid-East countries, United States oil companies have repeatedly opposed reduction of lead in gasoline despite the evidence that lead has harmful effects. While there is no direct evidence that inhalation of lead fumes leads to psychological damage, there is much greater recognition of the problem of lead poisoning, and lead screening programs for children increased markedly in the late 1970's (*Newsweek,* June 14, 1980). Symptoms of lead poisoning include weakness, constipation, indigestion, and a form of paralysis in the forearms and hands. According to Dr. John Gallogher of the U.S. National Center for Disease Control in Atlanta, Georgia, in 1980, 4 percent of the children screened were found to have lead toxicity. In 1976 200,000 tons of lead were added to the air, whereas in 1980 because of the Clean Air Act in the United States, only 90,000 tons were added to the air (*Newsweek,* March 29, 1980). Further, in 1982 it was decided to tighten federal limits on lead ore to decrease the amount of lead in the air by 31 percent over the next eight years (*Science,* August 20, 1982).

Fluorescent Lighting

In 1974, a group of researchers looked at the effects of standard flurorescent lighting on the behavior of children in regular class-rooms. One group of children were exposed to light from a standard fluorescent system, and another group of children were exposed to light from a full-spectrum system (that is, light that contains wavelengths similar to those of natural sunlight). It was reported that the children exposed to the full-spectrum systems showed greater reductions in hyperactive behavior than did children who were exposed to standard fluorescent systems. This report made sense to a number of people who had noticed that fluorescent lights often have a flicker that can be irritating. However, the flicker is usually due to a lamp that has begun to deteriorate. The question of interest, though, was whether a good fluorescent bulb would have a detrimental effect on children's behavior. My colleagues and I decided to reexamine this question because we felt the previous research had serious flaws which rendered their conclusion questionable.

In our study, the two lighting conditions were compared at a university laboratory school for children with conduct disorders and/or hyperactivity. Several factors were controlled in this study, but no difference was found in the children's hyperactive behavior under the two lighting conditions (O'Leary, Rosenbaum and Hughes, 1978).

In sum, fluorescent lighting does not appear to have an effect on the behavior of hyperactive and conduct disorder children.

Summary

Activity level and attention span are clearly influenced by heredity. Men with the chromosomal abnormality XYY, or "extra male" chromosome, are generally taller than the average man, but there is only suggestive evidence that men with the XYY chromosome are more aggressive than average. There is no clear evidence that aggression in children or adolescents is associated with levels of male hormones (testosterone).

"Minimal Brain Dysfunction" was seen by professionals as a cause of most hyperactive behavior. However, it has become clear that only five to ten percent of hyperactive children did have any brain injuries. Dietary concerns, such as the possible adverse effects of food additives and coloring, have become very popular, and groups like the Feingold Association have developed across the United States. However, only a very small percentage of young children appear to be adversely affected by food coloring and food additives or preservatives. Sugar intake in young children with behavioral problems has been associated with aggression, but more research is necessary to clearly document this association.

Eating lead paint chips or inhaling lead fumes can lead to serious neurological problems, and lead has now been eliminated from paint. The adverse role of lead in gasoline has been hotly debated, but in 1982 the U.S. government decided to decrease the amount of lead in the air by approximately 35 percent. Finally, fluorescent lighting was viewed as a cause of hyperactive behavior. While adults often rate fluorescent lights as annoying, there is no evidence that fluorescent lights cause hyperactivity in children or adults.

References

Feingold, B. F. *Why your child is hyperactive.* New York: Random House, 1975.

Fuller, J. L., & Thompson, W. R. *Foundations of behavioral genetics.* St. Louis, Missouri: C. V. Mosby Company, 1978.

Jarvik, L. F., Klodin, V. & Matsuyama, S. S. Human aggression and the extra Y chromosome. *American Psychologist*, 1973, *28*, 674–682.

Moyer, K. E. *The psychobiology of aggression.* New York: Harper & Row, 1976.

Needleman, H. L., Gunnoe, C., Leviton, A., Reed, R., Peresie, H., Maher, C., & Barret, B.S. Deficits in psychological and classroom performance of children with elevated dentine lead levels. *New England Journal of Medicine*, 1979, *300*, No. 13, 689–695.

Noel, B., Duport, J. P., Revil, D., Dussuyer, I., & Quack. B. The XYY syndrome: Reality or myth. *Clinical Genetics*, 1974, *5*, 387–394.

O'Leary, K. D., Rosenbaum, A. and Hughes, P. C. Fluorescent lighting: A purported source of hyperactive behavior. *Journal of Abnormal Child Psychology*, 1978, *6*, 285–289.

Prinz, R. J., Roberts, W. R., & Hartman, E. Dietary correlates of hyperactive behavior in children. *Journal of Consulting and Clinical Psychology*, 1980, *48*, 760–769.

Rapoport, J. L., Buchsbaum, M. S., Zahn, T. P., Weingarten, H., Ludow, C. & Mikkelsen, E. Dextroamphetamine: cognitive and behavioral effects in normal prepubertal boys. *Science*, 1978, *199*, 560–563.

Rose, T. L. The functional relationship between artificial food colors and hyperactivity. *Journal of Applied Behavior Analysis*, 1978, *11*, 439–446.

Rutter, M. Raised blood levels and impaired cognitive/behavioral functioning: A review of the evidence. Supplement to *Developmental Medicine and Child Neurology*, 1980, *22*, No. 1, 1–26.

Scaramella, T. J., & Brown, W. A. Serum testosterone and aggressiveness in hockey players. *Psychosomatic Medicine*, 1978, *40*, No. 3, 262–265.

Still, G. F. The Coulstonian lectures on some abnormal physical conditions in children. *Lancet*, 1902, *1*, 1008–1012.

Trites, R. L., Tryphonas, H., & Furguson, H. B. Diet treatment for hyperactive children with food allergies. In R. M. Knights and D. J. Bakker, *Treatment of hyperactive and learning disordered children*. Baltimore, University Park Press, 1980.

Walker, S. *Help for the hyperactive child*, Boston: Houghton Mifflin, 1977.

Willerman, L. Activity level and hyperactivity in twins. *Child Development*, 1968, *39*, 27–34.

Witkin, H. A., Mednick, S. A., Schulsinger, F., Bakkestrm, E., Christiansen, K. O., Goodenough, D. R., et al. Criminality in XYY and XXY men. *Science*, 1976, 547–556.

4

Social Causes of Aggression and Hyperactivity

In some societies aggression is held in high esteem, especially in men. In others aggression is viewed negatively, and it is rarely seen. More specifically, religious groups like the Quakers, Muslims, and Hutterites emphasize pacifism as a way of life. They encourage refusal to fight in the armed forces and generally decry violence of any sort. On the other hand, aggression is valued by certain gangs of teenagers in most Western societies. Often these teenagers are unable to derive pleasure and satisfaction from more accepted life styles. They are often school dropouts from economically disadvantaged backgrounds. Of course, not all aggression in Western societies is displayed by economically deprived teenagers. Aggression is often rewarded in the marketplaces, courtrooms, and negotiating tables throughout the world. We will review the multiple social causes of aggression in this chapter and the more poorly understood social causes of hyperactivity. Social causes refer to learning factors or events in a child's social environment which lead to hyperactivity and aggression.

In this chapter we will look at the most important social determinants of aggression and hyperactivity. Somewhat more space will be devoted to the causes of aggression than of hyperactivity, although the importance of learned behaviors for both aggressive and hyperactive children is critical.

The social causes of aggression, or the ways in which we learn aggression include:

rewards, modeling, stopping aversive conditions, frustration, punishment and erratic discipline, and marital discord.

Rewards for Aggression

Rewards for being aggressive are obvious in many competitive sports. To win a game of football, soccer, basketball, racquetball, or tennis, it helps to be aggressive. Boxing and wrestling clearly require aggression. As organized sports for children become more developed throughout the world, skill development will be emphasized, but any good coach knows that development of skill in these sports necessitates development of some aggressive behavior. Even a casual observer of practices and games in children's sports leagues will hear comments like, "Beat that guy to the ball, and use your shoulders to push him off you," (soccer); "Great job, Brian, you really creamed that guy!" (wrestling); "You have to hit that line like a truck and make sure the guy is down and not able to get free to tackle our running back," (football). In addition to instructions to be aggressive and words of encouragement and praise from the child's parents and family, there are patches a child can place on his or her jacket which indicate tournament wins. Finally, there are trophies for individual and team performances. In sum, there are many direct rewards for being aggressive in sports.

In fact, direct rewards for aggression are not limited to the sports arena. For example, direct observation of nursery school children indicates that aggression of children pays off more often than not. Patterson, Littman and Bricker (1967) observed 36 nursery school children over a nine-month period. They coded the consequences of the aggression into positive and negative categories, i.e., categories of behavior that would presumably reward (positive) or punish (negative) the aggression. The positive consequences for the aggressive behavior included the victim crying, being passive, and acting defenseless; the negative consequences included telling the teacher, retaliation, and teacher intervention. The results of their study showed that aggressive behaviors are generally followed by positive consequences. Furthermore, even children who are initially passive and unassertive often experience positive consequences for their aggression.

When these initially shy children counterattacked, their counterattacks were often successful, and their aggressive behavior increased markedly.

Rewards for aggressive behavior also occur between brothers and sisters. Consider an example of a case I saw several years ago of a woman who had grown up with an aggressive sister. The younger child, who always gave in to her sister, grew up to be a nice shy adolescent, whereas the older sister grew up to be known as "Bossy Betsy." Betsy was seen as a good student and one who often got the boys in junior high school. In high school, however, her bossy reputation caught up with her, and she found herself disliked by many students. The younger sister, Sara, was rarely asked out in junior high school but dated several boys frequently in high school. Unfortunately, Sara developed problems in her marriage because she was very unassertive, and her husband learned she was easy to boss around, just as her sister Betsy had done for years. For example, she did not tell her husband that she didn't want to have sexual relations even though she often was not interested. She rarely told him that she disliked his staying out late at night drinking because she hated to have him yell at her, saying, "I can do what I please as long as I can make it to work the next day."

This clinical example is given to portray the long-term effects of rewards for aggressive behaviors in childhood (i.e. Sara's rewarding Betsy's aggression by her submission). As parents, we should be careful to note that what appears to be desirable, docile behavior in the home and school may later have negative consequences. In brief, repeated dominant-submissive patterns in children should be watched and stopped if they become very characteristic of the children's interaction patterns. Rewards for aggression are also apparent when one looks at the types of interactions between parents and children. One often hears a father say, "I don't want to catch you hitting your brother, but if John Smith hits you at school, I want you to beat the hell out of him." While not all children will follow such parental imperatives, it is known that children praised for hitting do increase their assaultive attacks more than children who were not praised for hitting (Patterson, Ludwig, & Sonoda, 1961). Bandura and Walters (1963) summarized their work regarding positive reinforcement or rewarding of aggressive behavior in families in which they found that parents of aggressive boys permitted considerable aggression among brothers and sisters, and they explicitly rewarded their sons' aggression when it was directed at children outside the home. Interestingly, they also found that boys judged to be aggressive in school were not particularly aggressive toward their parents.

It is also worthwhile noting that teachers can unwittingly or unknowingly reward children's disruptive behavior by the way in which they respond to it. For example, Madsen, Becker, Thomas, Koser, and Plager (1968) found that if first grade teachers yelled, ''Sit down!'' at their children when they were out of their seats, they actually increased the amount of time they were out of their seats. That is, giving disapproving comments or commands following inappropriate behavior such as standing up in the classroom served to increase the very behavior the teacher wished to decrease. In a similar fashion, my colleagues and I (O'Leary, Kaufman, Kass, & Drabman, 1971) found that loud reprimands audible to most children in the classroom actually served to maintain or increase disruptive behavior of elementary school students. In contrast, a soft reprimand, i.e., a reprimand audible only to the student receiving the reprimand, served to decrease disruptive behavior. Although the disruptive behaviors noted above were not necessarily aggressive, the implication of the work is that teachers and parents can inadvertently reward undesired behavior. For example, teachers who simply yell, ''Cut it out!'' to their children when they are teasing and fighting may simply increase the level of fighting. Alternatively stated, attention, even though it is somewhat negative, may serve to reward rather than punish a child.

Modeling of Aggression

Children imitate their parents and friends almost constantly.

We often mistake the voices of teenage children for those of their parents' because their speaking styles—pace, timber, enunciation, and accent—are so similar to those of their parents'. As parents we may be annoyed by the desires of our children to wear the same clothes, have the same toys and sports equipment, and engage in the same activities as their peers. We shudder when our children repeat foul expressions or four-letter words which we may have inadvertently uttered in their presence.

The adverse effects of modeling are also seen, unfortunately, in the public arena. When hijacking of airplanes occurs, it often occurs in a series of incidents. More specifically, it appears that when a hijacking is reported in the news media, certain disturbed individuals are prompted to engage in hijacking. Publicizing famous people's use of drugs and alcohol also has an apparently detrimental effect on teenagers. Rock stars and movie stars have been notorious for their almost flagrant use and misuse of legal and illegal drugs. The problem prompted Kathy Lee Crosby, a television personality, to encourage entertainers to serve as better models for youth and to decry the use of drugs and alcohol (*Time*, 1980). Such action by Ms. Crosby is indeed highly commendable, because as we shall soon see, youths readily model peers and those they respect.

Now let us turn to some of the research on the effects of modeling on aggression. In the early 1960s, Bandura and his colleagues at Stanford University in California conducted a series of experiments which demonstrated how young children readily imitate aggressive models. Children who viewed movies of children behaving aggressively displayed more aggressive behavior in their classes than children who viewed movies without aggressive scenes. These experiments were classic in that they served to alert us to the very powerful effects of peer models.

Modeling effects in real life situations were shown by Lefkowitz, Eron, Walder & Huesman (1977) who evaluated the effects of exposure to TV violence. Lefkowitz and his colleagues collected data from 400 nine-year-old boys, including peer ratings, television viewing habits, and parental disciplinary practices. Ten years after the initial assessment, Lefkowitz and his colleagues collected similar data on the same 400 individuals who were then nineteen years old. For boys, exposure to TV violence at nine years of age was significantly related to aggressive behavior at age nineteen. That is, boys who watched a high level of TV violence at age nine were likely to be more aggressive at age 19 than boys who were not exposed to a high level of TV violence at age nine. The effects of modeling aggression are clear. Watching aggression by others in one's daily life and on television leads to the increased aggression in children.

In addition, there are apparent negative effects of observing self-inflicted aggression on television. In 1981, the National Coalition on Television Violence collected data indicating that eighteen persons shot themselves after seeing the television movie *The Deerhunter*. *The Deerhunter* depicted men playing Russian Roulette, a violent game involving placing a gun with one bullet to one's head and gambling that pulling the trigger would fire that bullet. In addition, an increase in suicide attempts was found to be related to watching television soap operas after a fictional soap opera character tried to take her life.

Unfortunately, efforts by consumer groups to curb TV violence have not been very successful. There were eight acts of violence per hour on prime time TV in 1972, and in 1982 there were still seven acts of violence per hour. Cartoon violence even increased during the same time period from 30 to 36 violent acts per hour (*NCTV News*, January, 1981; September 1982). One potentially useful method to decrease violence on TV is to boycott products which advertise programs containing high rates of violence. For example, when the Coalition for Better Television advocated boycotting products advertised on shows featuring sex and violence, Proctor and Gamble, TV's biggest customer, announced that it was pulling out of "50 TV movies and series episodes, including seven of the ten that Wildmon [head of Coalition for Better Television] has cited as 'top sex-oriented'." (*Time*, July 6, 1981).

Although some parent groups have produced changes in television practices, such as having "Family Viewing Time" during afternoon and early evening broadcasts in which violence and sex are monitored or eliminated, parents should play an active role in monitoring the television viewing habits of their own children. Certain children may be able to distinguish cartoons and fantasy aggression from real life aggression, and they may be able to distinguish the situations in which aggression is appropriate and inappropriate. Children with problems of impulse control, however, may be more easily influenced by TV violence than children who are able to control their emotions and behavior.

The Violence Stays When the TV Goes Off

As a large window on the world for young people with little worldly experience of their own, television is in a strong position to influence developing social attitudes. The consequences have long been a subject for debate, and now the debate can be fine-tuned.

A new government report analyzing hundreds of studies and publications over the last decade points to overwhelming scientific evidence that televised violence leads directly to aggressive and violent behavior in young viewers. As with studies linking cigarette smoking and cancer, explanations may still be incomplete, but the evidence leaves no room for doubt that the connection exists.

The report says the problem is not confined to school-age children and adolescents; even preschool children can be affected. One study found that heavy viewing of violent programs by three- and four-year-olds led to what the researchers regarded as unwarranted aggressive behavior during play.

The National Institute of Mental Health prepared the new report to update one issued by the surgeon general in 1972. The earlier one was unclear about whether the connection between television and aggression has long-term consequences; the new one holds that television's effects are both pervasive and cumulative.

The NIMH report cites studies showing that youngsters given to heavy television viewing are likelier to be more fearful, anxious and insecure than they otherwise might be. They're more inclined to harbor a distorted idea about the amount of violence in the world, and they're likelier to develop a lower threshold for violent behavior of their own.

Broadcasters owe the viewing public sober attention to the report and careful study of their own programing. Remedial action to limit violence, especially in programs normally watched by children, is their responsibility. But they're not the only ones who should act. Parents should recognize that the television set is no hazard-free plaything in their children's lives, but a powerful transmitter of values—sometimes undesirable ones. And they ought to see that their own values are given at least equal time.

—*Newsday*, Editorial, May 10, 1982

Stopping Aversive Conditions

Scram! Will you leave me alone! Find some kids your own age! Get lost! Get away from me! Go play in the street! We have all heard screams and orders like these from kids who want to get rid of other kids. Most often we hear such comments from teenagers as they try to shake loose their young brothers and sisters or younger friends. Sometimes the younger child does not even have to say anything to the older person. Just the presence of a younger child is often enough to make an older brother or sister angry.

One of the factors that appears to maintain aggressive behavior is stopping aversive or noxious situations. For example, Patterson and his colleagues found that a child will often attack to stop others' taunts and teasing (Patterson & Reid, 1970). It is important to note that aggressive children are often teased *more* than their nonaggressive brothers and sisters. This finding should lead parents of aggressive children to look at what prompts their children to be aggressive. Often one child in a family with behavior problems can become the butt of many jokes and taunts, and aggressive behavior becomes functional for the child because it helps the child defend him or herself against the teasing and taunting (Patterson & Reid, 1970).

Sometimes an older brother or sister can learn to be aggressive and bossy because he or she learns to stop what may appear to be aversive events from the younger brothers or sisters. For example, an older brother or sister may yell at the younger family members when they turn the radio on, when they horseplay in the kitchen, and when they spend too much time around the older brother and sister and their friends.

Frustration

Frustration has long been known to be a clear source of aggression. A classic monograph published in 1939 on aggression by Dollard, Doob, Miller, Mowrer, and Sears presented the view that aggression is a result of frustration. Dollard and his colleagues stated that aggressive behavior always presupposes the existence of frustration and that frustration always leads to some form of aggression. Frustration was seen both as a necessary and sufficient condition for aggression. While we now know aggression is only one of a number of alternative responses to frustration, the way children react to frustration relates directly to the way they have been raised.

What are the major sources of frustration for school-age children? Generally, problems in school, such as difficulty in completing work correctly or in completing work at all, become the largest sources of frustration for children. For some children, the structure and order of a classroom are too much with which to cope. In fact, one of the largest sources of referrals to mental health clinics is teachers in the early elementary school grades who say that their children cannot function in a classroom environment. Other children with poor social skills find that interactions with other children at recess and at play cause them the greatest problems. Not being chosen for games and being left on the sidelines can be especially frustrating for a child.

Frustration with family and marital problems over which a child has little or no control can also be especially trying for a child or adolescent. When children hear parents yell at one another about getting a divorce, the child may feel threatened and frustrated because there may be nothing he or she can do to make divorce less likely.

Punishment and Erratic Discipline

There is considerable evidence that parents who use severe punishment and who punish frequently are likely to have aggressive children. Sears, Maccoby and Levin (1957) interviewed approximately 400 mothers of five-year-old children and found that severity of punishment used by parents and extent of disagreement between parents was associated with aggression in the young children. Bandura and Walters (1959) interviewed mothers, fathers, and their aggressive teenagers and compared the results of these interviews to interviews of nonaggressive youths. Like Sears and his co-workers (1957), Bandura and Walters (1959) found that parents of the aggressive youth were more punitive, more often disagreed with each other, and were more likely to be cold and rejecting.

There are a number of studies which confirm the above conclusion. Severe punishment, general parent disagreements, hostility between parents, and rejection by parents is associated with aggression in children. Further, there is considerable evidence that aggression is a relatively stable characteristic. In fact, intelligence and aggression appear to be two of the most stable characteristics of children. Aggression at age five is clearly predictive of aggression at age ten, and aggression at age nine predicts aggression at age fourteen.

It is possible that strong parental punishment comes from having to cope with children's strong aggressive outbursts. Recent research indicates that children have clear effects on their parents, and we cannot simply infer that if high rates of childhood aggression are related to strong parental punishment, then the parental punishment leads to high rates of aggression. Strong disciplinary practices are more likely to be used by parents when a child is highly active, as illustrated by Long (1973). Parents were asked to watch videotapes of children with varying levels of activity and record the punishment they would give the child based on his or her behavior. Long found that parents were more likely to punish highly active children, even when they were doing the same activity as less active children.

Parents should not infer that because their child is more active or misbehaving than others severe punishment practices are justified. If you are a parent who is using frequent and severe punishment with your child, you should do your best to stop such action, and you should consult a psychologist, psychiatrist, or social worker.

Marital Discord

My colleagues and I have been looking at the relationship between conflict and childhood problems by assessing the marital conflict of the parents of children who came to our child psychological clinic at the State University of New York at Stony Brook. We predicted that marital discord would be associated with aggression and conduct problems of boys, but, to our surprise, marital conflict was associated with many problems of boys, not just conduct problems and aggression. More specifically, we found that marital problems, especially overt marital hostility, were associated with anxiety, immaturity, and personality problems of boys. On the other hand, marital problems were not consistently associated with problems of girls (Porter & O'Leary, 1980; Emery & O'Leary, 1982).

The association between marital problems and childhood problems has also been found by Rutter (1978) in England. In studying ten-year-old children on the Isle of Wright and inner London, Rutter found that parents with severe marital discord were more likely to have children with psychiatric disturbances than parents without marital problems. Interestingly, however, Rutter found that marital discord alone was not a sufficient condition to produce psychiatric problems in children. Marital discord had to be associated with *one* of five other stresses to produce a *severe* childhood problem. The five other stresses were: (1) overcrowding or large family size, (2) father holds an unskilled or semiskilled job, (3) mother has a depressive neurosis, (4) child has been placed in foster family or children's home, (5) father has had a legal offense.

It should also be emphasized that children with behavior problems can contribute to or accentuate marital discord. This issue becomes obvious when you repeatedly hear parents argue about how they should discipline a child or whether they should discipline the child at all for certain behavior. Of course, it is also the case that there can be a reciprocal relationship between marital discord and childhood problems.

The stress of being a parent of a normal child puts strain on a marriage, and it is well-recognized that the presence of the first child leads to a moderate but significant reduction in marital satisfaction. There is no body of research regarding the effects of children's psychological problems on marital satisfaction, but there is evidence that marital satisfaction of parents of children with physical handicaps such as spina bifida (a neurological problem) declines during the first nine years of the child's life. Further, the divorce rate of parents of children with spina bifida is higher than the average (Tew, Payne, & Lawrence, 1974).

The important point for a parent to recognize is that there often is an interaction between child and marital problems. Although the stress of having a child with serious physical problems such as spina bifida may not be as great has having a child with psychological or behavior problems, if you are concerned about the effects of your child's problem on your marriage, address these problems with a professional. Clearly not all child problems affect marital satisfaction, and not all marital problems affect child problems, but in many cases these relationships exist, and they should receive attention.

We have found that parents of children brought to psychological clinics are, on the average, less satisfied with their marriage than parents of a randomly-selected group of parents of children matched to the clinic group for age and education. However, at least one-third of the parents of the children brought to our clinic have very satisfactory marriages (Oltmanns, Broderick, & O'Leary, 1977).

Social Causes of Hyperactivity

Aggression has been the subject of serious psychological study for decades, whereas hyperactivity has only recently begun to receive such psychological attention. Hyperactivity, particularly in its extreme form, has long been viewed as an organic or physical problem. This view deterred researchers from searching for social causes of hyperactivity. However, as we shall see, there are a number of behaviors, which are probably learned, that characterize hyperactive children. For example, the following behaviors which distinguish hyperactive from non-hyperactive children presumably are influenced by learning: talks too much, leaves the class without permission, constantly demands candy, cannot tolerate delay, and has temper tantrums (O'Leary, 1978).

Deficient Teaching

Sometimes young children lack fine motor skills and patience because parents simply do not teach such behaviors. A former client of mine had a seven-year-old boy who appeared to have some difficulty sitting still and some difficulty coloring when he was three or four years old. The mother believed that he would grow out of his difficulty and that pushing him would simply magnify the problems she already had with him. Therefore, from the time the child was four he had little teaching or assistance in learning how to color, use scissors, print, or work with puzzles. In second grade, his teacher felt he was a bright but very immature boy who should repeat second grade.

It should be emphasized that this boy might have inherited a predisposition to be very active. His father stated that he himself was a hyperactive child. This belief, that his son's hyperactive-type behaviors were inherited, coupled with the belief that pushing the child would cause interpersonal difficulties between the mother and child, led to a *laissez-faire,* or hands-off, child rearing attitude.

Fortunately, his parents were able to see how such an attitude led to their child's problems in school, and they then spent 10 to 15 minutes each day with him in tasks that would increase his patience and fine motor skills. Such tasks need not resemble school tasks directly. Certain toys foster sustained attention, patience, and fine motor skills. A large number of electronic games exist which require both attention and eye-hand coordination. Other electronic games require that children remember certain musical sounds or patterns and that the child reproduce the sounds or patterns by pressing certain buttons.

Some children's lack of patience and fine motor control may well be due to more than simple lack of teaching. However, when no known neurological problems are apparent, parental encouragement to use toys that will foster attention, patience, and eye-hand coordination are recommended.

Modeling

The effects of teachers' modeling on impulsive styles was documented by Yando and Kagan in 1968. They showed that when normal children in first grade (ages six to seven) were exposed to impulsive or reflective teachers from the fall of the year to the spring, the children's response styles became more impulsive or reflective, respectively. In short, by the end of a school year, children exposed to teachers who displayed rapid response styles acquired a pattern of solving problems quickly and impulsively. Similarly, children who had teachers who solved problems slowly and carefully learned to solve problems more slowly. The children in this research were not hyperactive and the children's error rates were not altered significantly, but the study demonstrates how impulsive problem-solving approaches can be learned. As Yando and Kagan (1968) concluded, "First-grade children placed with experienced, reflective teachers became more reflective during the school year than those placed with impulsive teachers" (page 33).

It is also important to note their finding that experienced relfective teachers were those who showed the greatest impact on their students. These reflective teachers might also have given children in their classes encouragement for inhibition and delay of behavior throughout the school year, and we cannot conclude that modeling alone caused the children to change their response styles. Nonetheless, whether modeling itself or modeling plus encouragement and support for reflective problem-solving brought about the changes in the children's behavior, it is clear that problem-solving styles can be altered.

Quiet Versus Noisy Classrooms

It has been my impression that hyperactive children are easily stimulated and aroused by a wide variety of noises. Further, high and varied noise levels may lead to hyperactive behavior in diverse groups of non-hyperactive children. While study carrels do not seem essential for a hyperactive child, it does seem important for both parents and teachers to reduce general noises and distracting events (people walking by) in areas where the child is studying.

There have been recommendations by special educators to reduce extraneous classroom noises and sounds for hyperactive children. For example, Cruickshank (1975) recommended the use of three-sided cubicles that screen out extraneous sounds and sights, and individual study carrels have been used in some special classes for children with emotional and behavioral problems. Unfortunately, there is very little information on the effects of noise on the attention level of hyperactive children. Whalen and her colleagues at the University of California (Whalen, Henker, Collins, Finck & Dotemoto, 1979) compared regular classroom conditions, called quiet periods, with a noisy condition, e.g., a radio playing rock music from a local station. Hyperactive children were in a morning classroom setting in the summer and they were observed with a complex observational coding system. The noisy condition resulted in less task attention and more movement, verbalization, noise, and physical contact than the quiet condition.

Formal Versus Informal Classrooms

Charles Silberman and other advocates of the British Infant School, Open Classroom, or Informal Classroom approach have noted that one seldom, if ever, sees a hyperactive child in an informal school (Silberman, 1970). The apparent absence of hyperactive children in such schools would presumably have to be at least, in part, a function of the school program since hyperactive children would certainly have attended such schools.

In an effort to address this question, a physician, Dr. Jacob, an elementary school principal, Mr. Rosenbald, and I compared an informal classroom setting with a formal classroom setting. More specifically, we were interested in the effects of placing hyperactive children in a classroom with other nonhyperactive children where they were told to do certain tasks (e.g., arithmetic, reading or spelling) at certain times as compared to a classroom setting where they could engage in such activities when they chose to do so. There were also slight differences in the format of the school materials to enable our comparison to resemble an open versus formal school setting. What emerged from this research, as well as from related research by Flynn and Rapoport (1976), was that hyperactive children are less distinguishable from their nonhyperactive peers in the informal classroom setting than in the formal classroom setting.

Hyperactive children did not respond to the differences in the types of classroom environments whereas the nonhyperactive children did. That is, nonhyperactive children changed their behavior to fit the type of classroom atmosphere, but the hyperactive children did not. We should not conclude from this research, however, that hyperactive children profit more from informal than formal classroom environments. Many of the children in this evaluation had attentional and academic problems, and it is reasonable to believe that hyperactive children may need considerable classroom structure and skill training to help overcome their academic and social problems.

We can conclude that when there is not a strong need for completing tasks at a particular time and in a particular order, the hyperactive child should not be pushed into such regimentation. Such structure simply makes the hyperactive child seem unlike his classmates. Stated differently, a formal classroom environment may be very helpful to a hyperactive child academically, but the structure of organization of the classroom should not be rigidly imposed on the child. Strong regimentation seems simply to frustrate a hyperactive child. It seems very important that a hyperactive child have tasks assigned to him or her, and that practice in those tasks is very important. On the other hand, rigid structure or organization may backfire with a hyperactive child.

Negative and Positive Attention

Certain types of attention that we give to children may serve to increase the very behavior we want to get rid of. You may recall that we discussed work by Madsen and his colleagues earlier in this chapter in which it was found that if first grade teachers yelled "Sit Down" at their students when they were out of their seats, the students actually increased the amount of time they were out of their seats. More specifically, giving disapproving comments or commands following inappropriate behavior such as standing up in the classroom served only to increase the very behavior the teacher wished to decrease.

There have been very few studies assessing the effects of types of teacher attention on hyperactive children. At the Point of Woods Laboratory School at the State University of New York at Stony Brook, the effects of removing varied punishments were assessed. More specifically, a small class of eight hyperactive children had been attending quite well for their teacher; they attended approximately 70 percent of the time. However, when their teacher removed all types of punishers (reprimands, loss of minutes of recess, or being sent out in the hall for a few minutes), the children's level of attending dropped markedly over a five day period. However, when the teacher could again use various punishers, the level of attention again increased (O'Leary, Rosen & Joyce, 1980).

In brief, teachers of hyperactive children who use no negative consequences may encourage the hyperactive behavior. Since three types of punishers were removed simultaneously, we cannot tell which particular consequence removal was most critical in altering the level of the children's attending. What is important is that children may take advantage of a teacher if they feel there will be no negative consequences for their behavior.

Summary

Causes of aggression and hyperactivity in family, school, and social situations were discussed. Research on aggression has been much more extensive than research on hyperactivity, but sometimes both hyperactivity and aggression are clearly related in part to social factors. Individuals in the child's environment serve as models for both aggression and hyperactivity, and parents and teachers serve as important models for desired and undesired behavior. Parents may swear, act critically or aggressively, and children often imitate such behavior. Parents may act impulsively and rush from one task to another, and children may also imitate such hyperactive-type behavior.

Frustrations at home or school can lead to aggression. Severe punishment or erratic disipline can also lead to aggression. Hyperactivity can be the result of a failure to teach fine motor skills and patience. Some types of negative attention to undesired behavior such as commands to sit down can also lead to hyperactive-type behavior. One should not conclude that all punishers should be removed from a hyperactive child's environment, for when all punishers were removed from a classroom, the children's attention decreased markedly. Like most social behavior, however, attending to a task can be increased by praise and other forms of approval.

Noisy classroom environments lead to decreases in attention and increases in motor restlessness of hyperactive children. High levels of regimentation should be avoided for hyperactive children, but social and academic skills should be stressed. Skill teaching can be taught within environments that are informal or relatively free of regimentation.

Social causes of aggression and hyperactivity are apparent in many areas. However, as indicated throughout this book, the causes of hyperactivity and aggression are highly varied and a sensitive parent, teacher, psychologist, or physician should be alert to the multiple causes of these problems. When children's problems have multiple causes, they generally call for multiple interventions or treatments.

References

Bandura, A., Ross, D., & Ross, S. Imitation of film mediated aggressive models. *Journal of Abnormal Social Psychology,* 1963, *66,* 3–11.

Bandura, A., & Walters, R.H. *Social learning and personality development.* New York: Holt, Rinehart & Winston, 1963.

Cruickshank, W.M. The education of children with specific learning disabilities. In W.M. Cruickshank & G.O. Johnson (Eds.), *Education of Exceptional Children and Youth,* 3rd edition, Englewood Cliffs, New Jersey: Prentice Hall, 1975. 242–289.

Dollard, J., Doob, L.W., Miller, N.E., Mowrer, O.H. & Sears, R.R. *Frustration and aggression.* New Haven, Conn.: Yale University Press, 1939.

Emery, R., & O'Leary, K.D. Children's perception of marital discord and behavior problems of boys and girls. *Journal of Abnormal Child Psychology*, in press.

Flynn, N.M., & Rappoport, J.L. Hyperactivity in open and traditional classroom environments. *Journal of Special Education,* 1976, *10,* 285–290.

Jacob, R.G., O'Leary, K.D., & Rosenblad, C. Formal and informal classroom settings: Effects on hyperactivity. *Journal of Abnormal Child Psychology,* 1978, *6,* 47–59.

Lefkowitz, M.M., Eron, L.D., Walder, L.O., & Huesman, L.R. *Growing up to be violent.* New York: Pergamon, 1977.

Long, J.S. The effect of behavioral context on some aspects of adult disciplinary practice and affect. *Child Development,* 1973, *44,* 476–484.

Madsen, C.H., Becker, W.C., & Thomas, D.R. Rules, praise, and ignoring: Elements of elementary classroom control. *Journal of Applied Behavior Analysis,* 1968, *1* 139–150.

Madsen, C.H., Becker, W.C., Thomas, R.R., Koser, L., & Plager, E. An analysis of the reinforcing function of "sit down" commands. In R.K. Parker (Ed.), *Readings in educational psychology.* Boston: Allyn & Bacon, 1968.

Nation Coalition on Television Violence News, January, 1981. Decatur, Illinois.

O'Leary, K.D. The etiology of hyperactivity. Paper presented at the Second Annual Italian Behavior Therapy Association Meeting, Venice, Italy, June, 1978.

O'Leary, K.D., Kaufman, K.F., Kass, R.E., & Drabman, R.S. The effects of loud and soft reprimands on the behavior of disruptive students. *Exceptional Children*, 1970, *37*, 145–155.

O'Leary, S.G., Rosen, L.A., & Joyce, S. Removing negative consequences for undesired classroom behavior of hyperactive children. Unpublished manuscript, State University of New York, Stony Brook, New York, 1980.

Oltmanns, T.F., Broderick, J.E., & O'Leary, K.D. Marital adjustment and the efficacy of behavior therapy with children. *Journal of Consulting and Clinical Psychology*, 1977, *45*, 724–729.

Patterson, G.R., Littman, R.A., & Bricker, W. Assertive behavior in children: A step toward a theory of aggression. *Monographs of the Society for Research in Child Development*, 1967, *32*, Whole No. 113.

Patterson, G.R., Ludwig, M., & Sonoda, B. Reinforcement of aggression in children. Unpublished manuscript, University of Oregon, Eugene, 1961.

Patterson, G.R., & Reid, J.B. Reciprocity and coercion: Two facets of social systems. In C. Neuringer and J. Michael (Eds.), *Behavior modification in clinical psychology*. New York: Appleton-Century-Crofts, 1970, pp. 133–137.

Porter, B., & O'Leary, K.D. Marital discord and childhood behavior problems. *Journal of Abnormal Child Psychology*, 1980 *8*, 287–295.

Rutter, M. Isle of Wight studies, 1964–1974. *Psychological Medicine*, 1976, *6*, 313–332.

Sears, R.R., Maccoby, E.E., & Levin, H. *Patterns of child rearing*. Evanston, Illinois: Row, Peterson, 1957.

Silberman, C. *Crisis in the classroom*. New York: Random House, 1970.

Tew, B., Payne, H., & Lawrence, K.M. Must a family with a handicapped child be a handicapped family? *Developmental Medicine and Child Neurology*, 1974, *16*, 95–98.

Whalen, C.L., Henker, B., Collins, B.E., Finck, D., & Dotemoto, S. A social ecology of hyperactive boys: medication effects in structured classroom environments. *Journal of Applied Behavior Analysis*, 1979, *12*, 65–81.

Yando, R.M., & Kagan, J. The effects of teacher tempo on the child. *Child Development*, 1968, 39, 27–34.

5

Pharmacological and Dietary Treatments

History

The use of psychostimulant medication for the treatment of hyperactivity began in Providence, Rhode Island (U.S.A.), in 1937. At that time, Dr. Charles Bradley, a physician, published the first report of the effects of Benzedrine, a psychostimulant, on children with behavior problems. Dr. Bradley was the director of a home for children with severe behavior problems, and he prescribed Benzedrine to raise the blood pressure of some children in an attempt to rid them of headaches. While the Benzedrine did not improve the children's headaches, it appeared to help the children's school performance. More specifically, Bradley reported that the children showed ''a great increase in interest in school material,'' and the children called the medication ''arithmetic pills'' because they felt they could complete their arithmetic assignments more readily when they were taking the medication.

Possibly the most striking change in behavior during the week of Benzedrine therapy occurred in the school activities of many of these patients. Fourteen [of 30] children responded in a spectacular fashion. Different teachers, reporting on these patients, who varied in age and school accomplishment, agreed that a great increase of interest in school material was noted immediately. There appeared a definite ''drive'' to accomplish as much as possible during the school period, and often to spend extra time completing additional work. Speed of comprehension and accuracy of performance were increased in most cases . . . The improvement was noted in all school subjects. It appeared promptly the first day Benzedrine was given and disappeared on the first day it was discontinued . . . Fifteen of the 30 children responded to Benzedrine by becoming distinctly subdued in their emotional responses. Clinically in all cases this was an improvement from the social viewpoint . . . In this group

77

were some children who had expressed their irritability in group activities by noisy, aggressive, domineering behavior. Such children under the influence of the drug became more placid and easy-going (Bradley, 1937).

Bradley and an associate named Bowen conducted further work with Benzedrine because they were concerned by two factors. First, as soon as the children stopped taking the medication, they regressed to their previous level of school performance. Secondly, it was unclear how a stimulant medication such as Benzedrine could calm children with behavior problems that often involved overactivity. They reasoned that perhaps the medication imparted a sense of well-being and confidence to the children such that their problems and conflicts would no longer be so distressing to them. Nonetheless, Bradley did not advocate routine use of stimulant medication for children with behavior problems, and his reports were largely ignored. In fact, in the fifteen years following Bradley's original demonstration of the effects of an amphetamine on children with behavior problems, very few publications other than Bradley's appeared on this topic. As we shall see, however, in the 1960s and '70s, a great interest developed in medication for children's psychological problems, following several studies which demonstrated the utility of psychostimulant medication. By the mid-70s, psychostimulant medication became the most frequent treatment for hyperactivity in United States.

What is Psychostimulant Medication?

Psychostimulant medication has the *physiological* effect in children and adults of increasing heart rate, blood pressure, and central nervous system responsivity. In hyperactive children, such medications have the *psychological* effect of decreasing restlessness and activity level while increasing attention span. In adults, psychostimulants produce a marked feeling of euphoria or being "high," and they also increase energy levels and attention span (this is why amphetamines are sometimes referred to as "speed"). Unfortunately, psychostimulants are often used by individuals who drive long distances, and certain diners that cater to truckers often sell them illegally. In brief, with adults, psychostimulants are addictive and dangerous. Recent studies seem to indicate that psychostimulants are not addictive to children when medically monitored.

Incidence of Psychostimulant Treatment

There are approximately 600,000 to 700,000 children in the United States who receive psychostimulant medication for hyperactivity during the school year. Alternatively stated, while 5 percent of children in elementary school are hyperactive, approximately 2 percent of these children receive psychostimulant medication in the U.S.A. The percentage of school children receiving psychostimulant medication in Baltimore County, Maryland, increased from 1.07 percent in 1971 to 2.12 percent in 1977. In 1981 the percentage of children receiving such medication in Baltimore County was 2.6 percent, so there is evidence of some increase in the incidence of psychostimulant treatment for children in at least one large U.S. county since the early 1970s.

In some countries, very few children receive psychostimulant medication. For example, in Sweden, the government has limited prescription of psychostimulant medication for hyperactive children because of a growing concern in that country about drug abuse in young adults and teenagers. In England, both the diagnosis of hyperactivity and use of psychostimulant medication are much less frequent than in the United States. Further, information obtained during a visit I made to the People's Republic of China in 1982 indicates that few children are given psychostimulant medication there. My own discussions with professionals in South America and Europe reveals that use of psychostimulant medication varies greatly with locale and the attitudes of physicians, educators, and parents toward the prescription of medication for hyperactivity. My impression is that use of medication for hyperactivity is greater in the U.S.A. than in any other country, and my associates and I are currently involved in research that examines the use of medication for hyperactivity across different cultures.

Types of Medication for Hyperacitivity

The most frequently used form of medication for hyperacitity is Ritalin (trade name) or Methylphenidate (chemical name). Ritalin is a psychostimulant and has been used since 1956; it is used in approximately 82 percent of the cases where hyperactive children are given medication. The second most frequently used medication for hyperactivity is Dexedrine (trade name) or Dextroamphetamine (chemical name). This medication has been in use since 1937, and currently it is used in approximately 9 percent of the cases where hyperactive children are prescribed medication. Finally, Cylert (trade name) or Magnesium Pemoline (chemical name) entered the market for treatment of hyperactivity in 1975. It is used in approximately 6 percent of the cases where hyperactive children are given medication (Gadow, 1979).

Approximately 3 percent of hyperactive children receive tranquilizers such as Mellaril (Thioridazine) or Thorazine (Chlorpromazine). As might be expected, tranquilizers reduce restlessness and anxiety, but they impair attention span in hyperactive children. In addition, they decrease reaction time and impair motor performance. In general, tranquilizers are reserved for use with children who have severe emotional disorders or who are mentally retarded, and whose hyperactive behaviors are secondary to the severe emotional disorder or mental retardation.

Ritalin is the most frequently used medication for hyperactivity because it is almost immediately effective; the results can be seen within approximately 30 minutes after ingestion. The negative side affects of psychostimulants, such as appetite loss and sleeping problems, are less with Ritalin than with Dexedrine. Cylert, the newest medication, is given in spansule, or slow release capsule, form so that the medication effects last the whole school day. In comparison, Ritalin and Dexedrine often have to be taken twice a day to allow the medication to have an effect across the school day. Unlike Ritalin and Dexedrine, however, Cylert is not fast-acting. For Cylert to be effective, it is necessary for a chemical build-up in the bloodstream to occur, a process which usually requires three to four weeks. In addition, since Cylert is the newest medication for the treatment of hyperactive children, the side effects of the medication are not yet as well studied as are the side effects of Ritalin and Dexedrine.

Effects of Psychostimulant Medication

Cognitive tasks. It has been known for almost a decade that stimulant drugs lead to an improvement in hyperactive children on various laboratory tasks requiring cognitive ability. For example, when hyperactive children receive stimulant medication, they show enhanced performance on a task that requires sustained attention. This task, a Continuous Performance Test, involves having a child sit in front of a screen while various stimuli, such as letters and numbers, are rapidly presented in succession on the screen. The child is then asked to press a button each time a specific number follows a certain letter. For example, the child might be asked to press the button each time the number "2" follows the letter "A." When hyperactive children receive psychostimulant medication, they show improvement on this task compared to their performance before they received the medication.

Short-term memory performance is also enhanced when hyperactive children receive stimulant medication. For example, a child may face a screen while various arrangements of pictures are flashed on the screen. The child is then presented with a single object and asked to indicate whether the object appeared in the previous array of pictures. The child indicates his or her answer by pressing a button, and a light (green or red) indicates whether the answer was correct or incorrect. Of special interest is the fact that the dosage of stimulant medication is associated with degree of improvement on this task. Children do best on this short term memory task when they are given a relatively small dose of stimulant medication. When they receive doses of stimulant medication that are somewhat higher but within the range of commonly administered doses, the children actually do worse than before they received the medication. In brief, as indicated by several investigators (Sprague & Sleator, 1975; Swanson et al., 1978), at doses of medication that are quite common, the cognitive performance of hyperactive children on some tasks is impaired. In summary, at relatively low doses of psychostimulant medication, performance on cognitive tasks improves, but when the dose is increased, children's performance on these tasks deteriorates.

An important question often asked by parents about stimulant medication is: "Will my child remember what he learned or saw when taking medication, but forget these things when he is no longer on the medication?" Technically, the concern is whether there is "state-dependent learning," that is, whether the child remembers or learns only when he or she is in a medicated state. Actually, hyperactive children who had learned something while receiving stimulant medication do remember what they had learned when they are no longer receiving the medication. In brief, the children are not dependent upon the medicated state to remember what they learned.

Motor performance. The most striking effect of psychostimulant medication on hyperactive children is on their motor performance. In research studies, the positive effects of psychostimulants on motor performance have been seen on children's enhanced ability to keep a pen moving through a maze without hitting the edges of the maze, and on children's ability to balance a tilted board that rotates on a central shaft. More importantly, psychostimulants often have a pronounced positive effect on handwriting. Below are two examples of a hyperactive child's handwriting, the first taken when the child was not receiving Ritalin, and the second when the child was given Ritalin. In a recent study of children with serious handwriting problems, 50 percent of children who received Ritalin improved in their handwriting, while only 5 percent of the children receiving a placebo (a pill without active psychostimulant medication) showed improvement in their handwriting (Lerer, Lerer, & Artner, 1977).

Social behavior in the classroom. The effects of stimulant medication on social behavior in the classroom are such that both teachers and independent observers rate children as improved on characteristics such as impulsiveness, distractibility, and fidgetiness. One research study looked specifically at the differences in classroom social behavior between hyperactive boys receiving Ritalin and hyperactive boys receiving a placebo (Whalen et al., 1979). It was found that the hyperactive boys receiving Ritalin spent more time working on their assigned tasks, were less noisy in the classroom, displayed fewer high-energy episodes, and displayed less sudden or unexpected behavior than the hyperactive boys receiving no medication (placebo).

The graph below illustrates the relationship between medication dosage and social behavior in the classroom, as found in an additional study. The children's social behavior was measured using the Conners Teacher Rating Scale, which we discussed in Chapters 1 and 2. As you can see, as the level of medication increases, the children's behavior problems decrease. To better understand the dosage amounts, imagine a ten-year-old child who weighs 75 pounds; the dosages would be approximately 3.5 milligrams, 10.5 milligrams, and 26 milligrams.

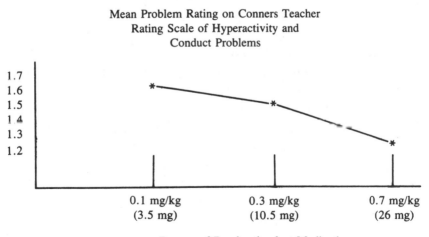

Mean Problem Rating on Conners Teacher
Rating Scale of Hyperactivity and
Conduct Problems

Dosage of Psychostimulant Medication
(Adapted from Sleator and von Neumann, 1974)

The problem with dosage effects on social behavior is that a physician or a teacher may observe little or no changes in social behavior and consequently increase the dosage level of stimulant medication until the classroom behavior is satisfactorily improved. However, from our previous discussion of the effects of psychostimulant medication on cognitive tasks, you will recall that a child's learning and memory ability is impaired at relatively large but commonly administered doses of psychostimulants. Thus, both parents and teachers should be alert to the possibility that increasing medication dosage in order to decrease the social problems in a classroom may be associated with an impairment of learning and remembering. Caution is always necessary in determining dosage level so that memory is not impaired. The dosage level for an individual child can be obtained by using a general dosage guide for a child's weight and then adjusting the medication to the particular child's reaction to it.

Activity level in classroom and the home. Parents often worry that children receiving psychostimulant medication will become or act like zombies: apathetic and listless kids. In general, this concern appears unwarranted for in fact, psychostimulant medication does not affect children's activity level in situations that are relatively unstructured, such as free play, recess, or playrooms. However, there is a very clear decrease in extraneous activity (for example, leg and finger tapping) and task-irrelevant behavior in classrooms (such as getting out of one's seat). Further, this decrease in activity level is accompanied by an *increase* in the child's attention span.

The absence of effects of psychostimulants on activity level in unstructured situations such as recess and free play raises the concern of parents that their child may not be helped by psychostimulant medication at home. In fact, while teacher ratings can readily detect whether a hyperactive child is on medication, parent ratings are generally not associated with whether a child is on active medication or a placebo. That is, parents often cannot reliably see a difference in their child's behavior after the child is put on, or taken off, medication. Part of the reason parents find it difficult to see positive changes in their children's behavior at home is that the major effects of the psychostimulants wear off in four to five hours. If a child receives medication at 7:00 A.M. and at noon, there will be some active effect of the medication for a short time after the child returns home from school, but for the majority of the time the child is at home, parents simply do not report positive effects on the child's behavior from the psychostimulant medication. Psychostimulants can not reasonably be given to children after school and in the evening because of the problems in sleeping a child would have if he or she received the medication after 3:00 P.M. Consequently, the practical problems of administering psychostimulants to children in the afternoon, as well as the parents' inability to see positive changes in their children's behavior should alert all parents that even when medication aids the child at school, the medication will generally not help address the child's behavior problems at home.

Side effects of psychostimulants. Stimulant medication frequently produces two side effects: sleeping and eating disturbances. Some children who receive psychostimulant medication find it difficult to fall asleep, and some children lose their appetite. Both of these side effects are generally controllable by reducing medication dosages, and they often subside after some initial adaptation to the medication. In addition, the side effects disappear rapidly if medication is totally discontinued.

The use of psychostimulants by adults to decrease appetite in order to lose weight is very controversial. As mentioned earlier, adults obtain a rush or a high with psychostimulants. Also, there is little evidence that these medications are effective in producing any long-term weight loss, and the drugs are addictive. Consequently, many medical associations such as the medical society ·in the county where I reside (Suffolk County, New York), have adopted resolutions agreeing that psychostimulants should not be prescribed for weight reduction. In fact, such medications have been placed on a list called Schedule II drugs to indicate their potential addictive nature with adults.

Other physical side effects of psychostimulants with children are weight loss, increased heart rate, and increased blood pressure. Children generally lose several pounds when they are placed on medication, and they have an increase in heart rate and blood pressure of approximately 10 percent. Two published reports in medical journals indicated that children on psychostimulants grew less than expected in terms of normal growth curves, especially with relatively high doses of dextroamphetamine. These reports have not been confirmed, but the reports may have caused enough concern that dosages now used are less than was the case previously. Further, the reports have caused greater interest in the suppressive effect of psychostimulants on growth hormones. In animals, psychostimulants decrease the production of growth hormones. Thus, when children are having a growth spurt, some physicians are especially concerned about continuing psychostimulants. This is one of the reasons psychostimulants typically are discontinued when the child approaches adolescence.

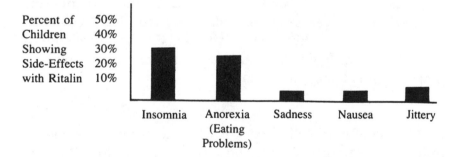

Side Effects
(Adapted from Conners, 1971).

There is a well-known article in child psychiatry and psychology called "The One Child, One Drug Myth." In it, Dr. Barbara Fish (1971) noted that no medication is "the" medication for all hyperactive children. In fact, a few children actually show an increase in problems when placed on psychostimulants, that is, they become more active, irritable, and agitated. Thus, if your child is on medication or if you are considering placement on medication, you should be alert to any unusual changes in your child's behavior. Most children show increases in attention and decreases in activity, and side effects, such as appetite suppression and difficulty in sleeping, can be controlled with decreased dosages. However, some children respond negatively and develop side effects which are not readily controlled with medication reductions. In brief, close observation of a child on medication is very important, especially when the drug is first started. Any suspected problems should be reported to the physician who prescribed the drug.

Who needs medication? There is considerable controversy over whether medication should be given to all, none, or some hyperactive children. A few quotes from some specialists in child psychiatry and psychology exemplify the diversity of opinion on the matter.

> As medications, the stimulant drugs are not remedies; they do not cure. The "treatment" they provide consists merely of squelching symptoms, and that temporarily. Sadly, it would seem that the pills that quiet children have had the side effect of quieting parents and teachers as well, and almost everyone else who is—or should be—concerned. (Walker, 1977).
>
> . . . medication is of the greatest importance in most instances . . . (medication is) the treatment that is both the best and sometimes the only treatment required . . . Psychotherapy may benefit the child . . . but unless he is medically treated it is very likely he will develop new problems. (Wender & Wender, 1977).
>
> I would not initially use pharmacological interventions with most hyperactive children because the behaviors that characterize the hyperactive syndrome are so dramatically, although fleetingly, changed by psychostimulants that the parents, teachers, and children may view the medication as a panacea, and we know that such is very far from the truth. (O'Leary, 1980).
>
> Because controlled studies have confirmed the symptomatic value of stimulant therapy, stimulants remain viable options for the man-

agement of hyperactivity and will so remain until effective *cures* are proved to exist. (Kinsbourne & Swanson, 1980).

It is likely that more and more physicians and psychologists will become reluctant to use or recommend psychostimulant medication with hyperactive children. This reluctance will stem in part from reports in the late 1970s that medication does not have long-term benefits, and from the failure of medication to produce any positive effect on standardized achievement tests. Medication has a powerful effect in terms of decreasing activity and increasing attention span, but as a sole treatment, it seems highly inadequate. The hyperactive child needs more than a medication that will make him or her calm and quiet. The child needs to be taught skills such as delaying gratification, tolerating frustration, and paying attention for longer periods of time. Such skills allow the child to be more in control of his or her own behavior.

Who responds positively to psychostimulants? Approximately 70 to 80 percent of hyperactive children show marked improvement in their behavior in the classroom when they are placed on some psychostimulant medication. Sometimes a child may not respond to one psychostimulant (e.g., Ritalin), but he or she may respond to another (e.g., Cylert). More importantly, a child may develop side effects with one psychostimulant medication but not with another. Generally, small doses of medication are given, and optimal levels of medication are decided according to a child's body weight.

While it is impossible to predict very precisely which hyperactive children will respond positively to medication, there are now some indications from research regarding which children will be good responders. Hyperactive children with abnormal EEG patterns and neurological soft signs (e.g., problems in coordination, writing, drawing, and balance) appear to show the most positive responses to psychostimulants. In addition, hyperactive children with strong attention deficits more frequently respond to psychostimulants than those with minor attentional problems (Barkley, 1981).

Do hyperactive children become addicted to psychostimulants? In 1970, a report in the *Washington Post*, a major newspaper in the United States, raised very serious concern about the high level of prescriptions of psychostimulants for children. In particular, it indicated that 5 to 10 percent of the children in elementary school in Omaha, Nebraska, were receiving psychostimulants. This report was erroneous, but it prompted a Congressional hearing on the use of psychostimulants with children. A major concern of the investigation was the potential addictive properties of psychostimulants with hyperactive children. When hyperactive children stop taking psychostimulants, a few children show strong short-term withdrawal effects exemplified by exacerbation of their problems (e.g., restlessness, low frustration tolerance), but most do not show these effects. Even the few who do show such effects have only temporary problems after the drug is withdrawn. Adolescents who receive psychostimulants as children are no more likely to depend heavily on drugs (e.g., tranquilizers, stimulants) than the general population of adolescents (Gadow & Sprague, 1980; Kramer & Loney, 1982). Of special interest is the report often heard from hyperactive children that they would like to stop taking the medication. In fact, even though about half of hyperactive children report that the medication helps them, at least 40 percent dislike receiving the medication and want to stop taking it.

Whenever a hyperactive child receives psychostimulants, the administration should be carefully monitored. When there is a teenage brother or sister of the hyperactive child in the family who has a history of drug or alcohol misuse and who knows about the effects of the psychostimulants, the medication should be guarded carefully because the teenager may be tempted to take the psychostimulants to get a quick "high."

Coffee. Some visitors to Mexico and South America feel that there are few hyperactive children in those countries because the children regularly drink *cafe con leche*, i.e., thick coffee with milk. Whether there are fewer hyperactive children in Mexico and South America is not clear, but it is clear that coffee contains a psychostimulant, and it has been known for years that coffee enhances attention and motor performance.

A physician, Dr. Schnackenberg of Columbia, South Carolina, observed that with hyperactive children who had problems taking psychostimulant medication, coffee appeared to be a good alternative. However, several controlled studies comparing the effects of Ritalin to coffee with hyperactive children showed Ritalin to be clearly superior to coffee in controlling impulsivity and hyperactivity. Further, since there is a correlation between coffee drinking and heart attacks in adults, it is not generally advisable to give a child the amount of coffee (two to three cups a day, or 200 to 300 milligrams of caffeine) that is necessary to have an effect on the child's behavior.

Tranquilizers. With extreme cases of aggressive or hyperactive children, tranquilizers such as Thorazine and Stelazine are sometimes used. While these tranquilizers are not habit-forming in children, they often have the unfortunate side effect of producing sleepiness and inattention. These soporific effects are especially apparent in the early stages of treatment.

Other side effects that are problematic are allergic reactions to the medication, and susceptibility to irritation by the sun (i.e., rashes or sunburns). Finally, if large dosages are required to deal with the aggression or hyperactivity, muscular stiffness, shaking, and trembling may develop.

In summary, tranquilizers are used in a very small percentage of children who are hyperactive and or aggressive, and there are several negative side effects often associated with their use.

Dietary Treatments. Concern about health and fitness has become a worldwide issue. In turn, concern about what we eat has become a highly discussed topic in professional journals and most importantly magazines and newspapers. In one way or another, we are constantly bombarded with the message "You are what you eat." This message is probably worthwhile in many ways but it also has disadvantages. It presents problems because many people focus on food and drink as primary or sole causes of their problems when they need to look elsewhere for causes and cures.

Cancer and heart disease are two major causes of death, and it has only been recently recognized that dietary factors can lead to cancer and heart disease. For example, eating certain additives such as nitrites (preservatives in bacon, ham, and poultry products) was seen as a possible cause of cancer in 1978, but in 1980 a United States government panel decided that it was unnecessary to ban nitrites on the grounds that it might cause cancer. Ingesting large amounts of salt is clearly known to be associated with high blood pressure and heart problems, and cholesterol is seen as a potential cause of heart problems. (The negative role of cholesterol has been questioned recently, but the tremendous amount of publicity paid to it has heightened the awareness of the public regarding dietary role in health and disease.) Pressure from consumer groups in the United States and Western Europe has led to regulations that food and beverage processors list all ingredients in their products. In turn, skepticism about artificial flavors and chemical additives has become rampant. My purpose here is not to review research on varied additives in food as they may relate to health problems. Instead, I simply wish to emphasize that the climate is ripe for the public to expect that dietary factors may cause hyperactivity and aggression. In the chapter "Biological and Physiological Causes of Aggression and Hyperactivity" we discussed how certain dietary factors may lead to problematic behaviors. We will here review whether changes in diet can lead to decreases in problematic behavior.

The Feingold Diet. Dr. Benjamin Feingold, an allergist from California, wrote a book, *Why Your Child Is Hyperactive*, in 1975. As noted in an earlier chapter, he claimed that the causes of hyperactivity could be found in artificial food coloring, especially red and yellow colors, and salicylates or natural aspirin-like compounds in fruits and vegetables.

The Feingold diet or variations thereof has been tried with both normal and hyperactive children. Most of the best controlled studies of the effects of food additives provide very little evidence that there is an adverse effect resulting from use of food dyes, salicylates, and flavorings (Conners, 1980). In one of the best controlled studies, Swanson and Kinsbourne (1980) admitted children to a hospital where diet could be controlled and where food coloring was adjusted to reflect levels that were at the *high* end of the daily average consumption. More specifically, they used two daily doses of food dye, 100 milligrams and 150 milligrams, and they found that children's learning was adversely affected by ingesting the food coloring.

Dr. Keith Conners, a research pioneer in evaluating the effects of psychostimulant medication and diet on hyperactive children, wrote a book, *Food Additives and Hyperactive Children* (1980). Conners conducted several studies on the Feingold diet or variations thereof. His comments are especially interesting because he conducted some of the best research evaluations in the diet area himself. He concluded as follows:

"On the basis of all the evidence available at this time, in answer to the question, "Is there anything to Dr. Feingold's hypothesis?" one might answer, "Yes, something—but not much and not consistently." As far as Dr. Feingold's *diet* is concerned, the facts show repeatedly that parents and teachers rate the children as improved after children are placed on the diet. Just as Feingold claimed, at least 50 percent show such improvement, but these changes appear to be due largely to placebo phenomena or other nonspecific factors." (p. 107)

Alternatively stated, the changes seen by parents of children on the Feingold diet may be due to parents' *expectations* that the children should improve. Children placed on placebo diets (diets that do not involve any changes that would occur with the Feingold diet) show as much improvement as children on the Feingold diet. Nonetheless, Conners noted that a "rather small number of children—perhaps less than five percent of those who are genuinely hyperactive—have some specific sensitivity to the artificial colors." He further noted that little research money is spent on factors affecting growth and development of children and that Feingold is owed a debt of gratitude for focusing attention on an important issue.

Even if only a small percentage of hyperactive children are

influenced by the Feingold diet, Feingold raised a very important question for us to consider. In brief, he asked why should we have food colorings in almost all our foodstuffs. Certain countries such as Italy have eliminated all dyes in food. On a recent visit to Italy, I was surprised to find that the prominent breath freshening mints, *Tic Tacs*, were all white or off-white. The cinnamon mints were not red as they are in Canada, the United States, and Mexico, and the peppermint mints were not green in Italy as they are in many North American and Western European countries. The Italians did not eliminate dyes from foodstuffs because of concern about hyperactivity. Instead, their concern was about *possible* cancer that might develop from ingesting foods with dye. In any case, the Italians do not seem to find their food less tasty without color; the colors or dyes are simply added for aesthetic reasons.

A very striking example of the role of food dyes in our life was made by Dr. Bernard Weiss of the University of Rochester at a National Science Foundation meeting in Williamsburg, Virginia (March, 1980). Weiss showed two slides to a large audience of scientists from diverse backgrounds including nutritionists, toxicologists, pediatricians, psychologists, and psychiatrists. The first slide showed a popular dog food chow with many colored bits. Dr. Weiss then said, "Now I'll show you what the dog sees." A slide then appeared with the same dog food, but the food simply appeared in shades of gray, white, and black. He then quickly said, "The dogs are color blind! And the colors are placed in the dog food for you, the consumer."

Dr. Weiss' point is well taken. Even if eating the food colors do not show that hyperactive children's behavior is adversely affected, one wonders why we should have the artificial colors in our food. If colors are added only to make the food more attractive, then we probably should look at natural ways of presenting foods that make them appear more pleasing.

Food Allergies. Certain substances such as cows' milk, chickens' eggs, and cereals often cause allergic reactions. A group of Canadian investigators (Trites, Tryphonas, and Ferguson, 1980)

examined 90 hyperactive children for the presence of food allergies. Blood sera were sampled for specific antibodies against
43 food abstracts. There was an association between number of
allergies and the teacher's rating of hyperactivity. In addition,
there was a clear association between number of allergies and
teacher ratings of hyperactivity. Even though this association
was found, it is important to note that about half of the hyperactive children did not have any allergic reactions. Further, a
diet change involving the specific substances to which the child
was allergic did not result in any greater improvement than a
placebo diet. It thus appeared that a small portion of hyperactive
children may have hyperactive behavior associated with food
allergies, and some case studies indicated that a few children do
respond positively to elimination of foods to which they have
shown allergic reactions. The particular foods for which a clear
positive allergic reaction (at least a score of 2 out of 4 on the
allergen test) was shown in these hyperactive children were as
follows: chicken, 16 percent; beef, 14 percent; oat, 14 percent;
rye, 7 percent. None of the other foodstuffs checked showed a
clear allergic reaction in more than 5 percent of the hyperactive
children. Practically speaking, parents need not worry very much
about their child's hyperactivity being the result of allergic reaction to specific foods.

Sugar Reactions. While there is little evidence that red and yellow
dyes, salicylates, or allergens affect hyperactive behavior of large
groups of children, there is evidence that the amount of sugar
or sucrose consumed by hyperactive children does influence the
level of their aggression and hyperactive behavior. Prinz, Roberts, and Hartman (1980) had parents of four- to seven-year-old
hyperactive children keep detailed food diaries. Parental records
indicated time of day, place where food was eaten, description
of food or beverage, type of food preparation, and amount consumed. The children were video-taped through a one-way mirror
while in a playroom alone with a variety of toys. The diets and
behavior of the hyperactive children were compared to a control

group of nonhyperactive children who were obtained via community advertisements.

Aggression and restlessness of the hyperactive children was clearly related to the amount of sugar consumed and to the ratio of sugar consumed relative to the amount of nutritional foods consumed. On the other hand, sugar consumption did not relate to aggression or restlessness in the control children. The only relation between sugar consumption and activity level was seen in a measure that reflected movement from one part of the room to another. It was interesting that the sugar intake did not differ between hyperactive and control children. Further, the hyperactive children did not differ from control children in terms of the number of foods consumed that were not permitted on the Feingold diet. The most important message a parent can glean from this work is that sugar in high amounts can aggravate hyperactive children.

Summary

In hyperactive children, psychostimulant medication has the effect of decreasing activity level, increasing attention span, and improving motor performance. The practice of prescribing psychostimulant medication for children with behavior problems varies widely from country to country. It appears that the use of psychostimulant medication is greater in the U.S.A. than in most other countries. Approximately 2 percent of the elementary school children in the United States receive psychostimulant medication.

At relatively low doses of psychostimulant medication, the performance of hyperactive children on cognitive tasks improves. However, as the dose increases to levels that are commonly given to hyperactive children, performance on cognitive tasks deteriorates. Social behavior of hyperactive children in their classrooms is improved when psychostimulant medication is given to the children. However, parents often see no change in their child's behavior at home as a result of the medication. The two major side effects of psychostimulant medication are sleeping and eating disturbances. These and other more infrequent side effects are generally controllable by reducing the medication dosage, or they often subside after an initial adaptation to the medication.

Recent studies indicate that hyperactive children do not become addicted to psychostimulant medication. However, because of reports in the late 1970s and early 1980s it seems likely that physicians and psychologists in the U.S. will become more reluctant to use or recommend psychostimulant medication with hyperactive children. This reluctance stems in great part from the failure of the medication to show long-term benefits and from the absence of positive effects on standardized achievement tests.

It has become evident that certain foodstuffs can effect us adversely, and the Feingold diet provided a clear impetus to study the relationship between hyperactivity and foodstuffs. While the behavioral effects of consuming artificial colors and salicylates appears to be very minimal at levels usually ingested by children, at high levels, artificial colors appear to affect behavior adversely. The most reasonable conclusion one can draw from many studies is that a very small percentage of hyperactive children are negatively affected by artificial coloring or food preservatives at the usual amounts ingested. Nonetheless, the only positive effect of food dyes is an aesthetic one, and countries such as Italy have eliminated food colorings without any important effect on the Italians' eating habits.

Allergic reactions of a small percentage of hyperactive children are observed with chicken, beef, oats and rye. Despite the clear allergic reactions observed on blood sera testing, dietary changes do not produce clear reductions in hyperactive behavior. In brief, while there is an association between hyperactivity and allergic reactions, elimination of the foodstuff to which the child is allergic does not necessarily lead to a reduction in hyperactivity.

Finally, sugar ingestion in hyperactive children does relate to both aggression and hyperactivity, and parents of hyperactive children should monitor the amount of sugar consumed by their children.

References

Barkley, R.A., Hyperactive children: a handbook for diagnosis and treatment. New York, N.Y.: Guilford, 1981

Bradley, C. The behavior of children receiving Benzedrine. *American Journal of Psychiatry*, 1937, *94*, 577–585.

Connors, C. Recent drug studies with hyperkinetic children. *Journal of Learning Disabilities*, 1971, *4*, 476–483.

Conners, G. K. *Food additives and hyperactive children*. New York: Plenum, 1980.

Feingold, B. F. *Why your child is hyperactive*. New York: Random House, 1975.

Fish, B. The "one child, one drug" myth of stimulants in hyperkinesis: Importance of diagnostic categories in evaluating treatment. *Archives of General Psychiatry*, 1971, *25*, 193–202.

Gadow, Kenneth. *Children on medication: A primer for school personnel.* Reston, VA: Council for Exceptional Children, 1979.

Gadow, K.D. & Sprague, R.L. An anterospective follow-up study of hyperactive children into adolescence: Licit and illicit drug use. Paper presented at meeting of American Psychological Association, Montreal, September, 1980.

Kinsbourne, M., & Swanson, J. M. Evaluation of symptomatic treatment of hyperactive behavior by stimulant drugs. In R. M. Knights & D. J. Bakker (Eds.), *Treatment of hyperactive and learning disabled children*. Baltimore: University Park Press, 1980.

Kramer, J. & Loney, J. Childhood hyperactivity and substance abuse: A review of the literature. In K.D. Gadow & I. Bialer, (Eds.), *Advances in learning and behavioral disabilities,* Vol. 1. Greenwich, Conn.: JAI Press, 1982.

Lerer, R. J., Lerer, P. M., & Artner, J. The effects of methylphenidate on the handwriting of children with minimal brain dysfunction. *Journal of Pediatrics*, 1977, *91*, 127–132.

O'Leary, K. D. Pills or skills for hyperactive children. *Journal of Applied Behavior Analysis*, 1980, *13*, 191–204.

Prinz, R. J., Roberts, W. A., Hartman, E. Dietary correlates of hyperactive behavior in children. *Journal of Consulting and Clinical Psychology*, 1980, *48*, 760–769.

Sleator, E. K., & von Neumann, A. Methylphenidate in the treatment of hyperkinetic children. *Clinical Pediatrics*, 1974, *13*, 19–24.

Sprague, R. L., & Sleator, E. K. What is the proper dose of stimulant drugs in children? *International Journal of Mental Health,* 1975, *4,* 75–104.

Swanson, J., Kinsbourne, M., Roberts, W., & Zucker, K. Time-response analysis of the effect of stimulant medication on the learning ability of children referred for hyperactivity. *Pediatrics,* 1978, *61,* 21–29.

Swanson, T. M. & Kinsbourne, M. Food dyes impair performance of hyperactive children on a laboratory learning test. *Science,* 1980, *207,* 1485–1486.

Trites, R. L., Tryphonas, H., & Ferguson, H. B. Diet treatment for hyperactive children with food allergies. In R. M. Knights & D. J. Bakker (Eds.), *Treatment of hyperactive and learning disordered children.* University Park Press, Baltimore, Maryland, 1980.

Walker, W. *Help for the hyperactive child.* Boston: Houghton Mifflin Co., 1977.

Wender, P.H. & Wender, E.H. *The hyperactive child and the learning disabled child.* New York: Crown Publishers, Inc., 1978.

6

Psychological Treatments

All children with problems of hyperactivity and aggression can benefit from their parents' understanding of their problems. In part, this understanding can come from concrete knowledge of the causes of their problems. It is my hope that you have obtained such understanding from reading the chapters on causes of aggression and hyperactivity in this book. Understanding the causes of a problem, however, does not always lead to knowledge about how best to treat the problem. Therefore, this chapter will be devoted to providing information for parents, teachers, and relatives of hyperactive and aggressive children that will aid them in the management of the children's problems. In addition, evaluations of psychological therapies and educational programs will be presented to provide a potential consumer of such services with evidence about the effectiveness of these programs.

In my opinion, parental participation is necessary in the psychological treatment of children. When parents participate in a child's treatment, they should receive information from the professional treating the child about psychological principles that can be used effectively with children who have problems of aggression and hyperactivity. In fact, in my opinion, any psychologist or psychiatrist who treats a child and does not provide aid to the parents about how to deal with their child is not providing a good service. Psychological therapies for aggressive and hyperactive children that have combined psychological consultation for the child *and* the parents have proven to be quite effective, and these programs will be described in this chapter. Even if you can not find a psychologist or psychiatrist who provides such programs, you can learn about how to deal with your child from reading about the programs.

In particular, in this chapter I will discuss behavior therapy, psychotherapy, and educational therapy or tutoring. These three interventions are the major non-pharmacological or non-drug methods for treating aggressive and hyperactive children. Rather than describe the theories regarding these treatments, I will describe what procedures are used by therapists and teachers who use these interventions. Finally, some commentary will be given regarding the effectiveness of these interventions.

Behavior Therapy

In the mid 1960s, an approach to treating children's psychological problems gained the attention of mental health professionals in England and the United States. This approach, called behavior therapy, has now gained considerable prominence throughout the world, and psychologists and psychiatrists can now receive training in behavior therapy in most countries. Behavior therapy is the application of learning principles in the treatment of psychological, educational, and social problems.

Behavior therapy with the family. Dr. Gerald Patterson of the University of Oregon in Eugene, Oregon, is a pioneer in the treatment of aggressive children. He has been treating aggressive children and their parents since the mid 1960s, and his work has been replicated in England by Martin Herbert. Further, Patterson and Guillion's teaching manual for parents, *Living with Children*, has been translated into Dutch, French, German, Spanish, and Swedish. Patterson's initial work involved repeated case studies with aggressive children, and later, large-scale evaluation programs of his treatments for aggressive children and their parents.

The Patterson treatment program for aggressive children, usually boys between the ages of 10 to 12 years, generally included emphasis on the following principles (Patterson, Reid, Jones, and Conger, 1975):

1) Reward desired behavior. Any behavior that a parent desires should be rewarded or reinforced. Thus, cooperative behaviors such as sharing, requesting aid rather than demanding help, and saying "thank you" should be praised or receive some

clear positive result, e.g., a pat on the back, a wink, or a hug.

2) Ignore undesired behavior. When a child has many behaviors that annoy a parent, it is pure folly to attempt to try to punish all of these behaviors. For example, when a child yells too much in the house, fails to comb his or her hair, swears, teases his or her brothers and sisters, hits his or her friends, and fails to bring homework home, parents will get hoarse and worn out if they try to consistently punish all of these behaviors. Instead, a parent must decide which behaviors are most important to change, and which behaviors can be ignored. If there are many undesired behaviors, it is best to ignore some and focus on two or three problems that cause greatest concern. Trying to give a child feedback on many undesired behaviors at one time is impractical and usually ineffective.

3) Punish undesired behavior. Some behaviors such as hitting and swearing require firm consequences that are likely to lead to cessation of the behavior. Such consequences might be isolation of a child in his or her room for a fixed period, removal of a child from a preferred activity (e.g., a family game or a game in school), or restriction from a privilege the child usually enjoys. Often, however, parents threaten, warn and argue with their children about undesired behavior. Whenever a parent tells me there is lots of arguing, I generally infer there is too little action. That is, lots of yelling and arguing generally means a parent is not administering enough consistent consequences for the undesired behavior.

Patterson and his colleagues (Patterson & Fleischman, 1979) have found that when there is an aggressive child in a family, the mother, brothers and sisters of the target child (the child referred for treatment) are more coercive than mothers and siblings in families without a child referred for treatment of aggression. By coercive, Patterson means that the family members often engage in verbal or physical attacks and threats as a way of changing each other's behavior. The findings regarding coercion have prompted Patterson and his colleagues to be alert to the possibility that the "aggressive child" may be the subject of attacks by family members and that some of the aggressive behavior may arise from the child's attempts to defend him or herself. In short, this analysis should make parents aware that part of the child's aggressive behavior may be maintained or supported by the child's discovery that the aggression leads to termination of others' attacks (e.g., teasing, goading, criticism).

Patterson has been quite successful in treating elementary school children, and his methods have been used by other investigators in many places. However, in addition to the types of treatment approaches we have described for young children, parents of older children and adolescents must learn to resolve family conflicts by discussing problems. Older children and adolescents do not respond to simple rewards and punishment with minimal reasoning; they need to participate with their parents in the problem-solving process. Problem-solving has been implemented successfully with adolescents and their parents according to the following four-step model (Foster, Princz, & O'Leary, in press):

1) Define the problem.
2) Generate alternative solutions without evaluation.
3) Evaluate alternatives by projecting positive and negative consequences, including compromise and choice of solution(s) to try.
4) Plan to implement the agreed-upon solution.

This model is deceptively simple; the level of emotional involvement plays a key role in the ability to implement this problem-solving approach. Therefore, a therapist typically aids a family or a parent and a teenager in starting discussions with relatively minor problems, and then progresses in a gradual fashion to more emotion-laden issues. As this progression occurs, the parent and adolescent are given feedback from the therapist about constructive communication (e.g., good listening, correct restatement of what the other person said), and destructive communication styles (e.g., name calling, repeated criticism, avoiding the issues).

Although we have been discussing treatment of aggression in

the home, there is also some evidence that conflict in the homes of hyperactive children can be reduced when a behavior therapy approach is used or when there is an emphasis on enhanced communication between parent and the child (Dubey, S. O'Leary, & Kaufman, 1983). This communication emphasis included the following types of guides for parents:

1) Use "I" statements rather than "You" statements. That is, state how you feel yourself rather than making inferences about how your child feels. For example, it is better to say, "I get discouraged when I see your breakfast dishes on the table every day" rather than, "You are deliberately trying to get me upset by leaving your breakfast dishes on the table every day."

2) Listen carefully and try to be able to restate what the person speaking has said. Parents can learn a great deal about a child's feelings if they simply listen more to their children. They can learn about their children's concerns, fears, and worries, as well as their likes and desires.

3) Invite the child to talk.

4) Do not interrupt the person speaking.

5) Acknowledge that you heard a comment.

A key factor in the communication training is "active listening," a technique whereby the receiver tries to understand what it is the speaker is feeling or what the message means. The communication emphasis with adolescents is critical because adolescents often feel that their parents do not understand them.

The behavior therapy approaches outlined have proven to be successful in many studies; families in treatment have greater change than families who do not receive such treatment (Patterson & Fleischman, 1980; Alexander & Parsons, 1973; Foster, Prinz, & O'Leary, 1980). More specifically, problems of aggression in the home have clearly diminished with treatment and there is some evidence that the treatment effects persist. Both better communication and better use of rewards, punishments, and reasoning can lead to a decrease in undesired behavior and an increase in desired behavior.

Behavior therapy in the school. Both aggressive and hyperactive children often have serious problems in school. In fact, most hyperactive and aggressive children have social problems, and approximately 75 percent have academic problems. Behavior therapy procedures in the classroom are similar to those in the home, although the emphais is on teacher-pupil interactions instead of parent-child interactions. This section on behavior therapy in the school is written largely with the teacher in mind, but a parent reading this section can also gain an understanding of how hyperactive and aggressive children can be successfully treated in the classroom.

Behavior therapy programs in regular classrooms where one or two children are aggressive or hyperactive have included the following interventions:

1) Praise and support of appropriate behavior. This general procedure means that appropriate behavior should receive some positive reaction from the teacher, such as a hug, a wink, a pat on the back, a smile, or verbal praise. Praise can also be in the form of little notes, slogans, or happy faces written on a completed assignment (e.g., "I'm proud of you, and I'm not lyin' " with a picture of a lion).

2) Ignore inappropriate behavior. Certain behaviors such as turning around in one's chair, fidgeting, and calling out answers without first raising a hand, can be ignored. To be effective, however, ignoring should be combined with praising appropriate behavior. Ignoring alone is not likely to be effective (Madsen, Becker, & Thomas, 1968) because classmates support disruptive behavior by their attention to it. The combination of praise and support of appropriate behavior has been shown to be effective in classrooms throughout the world, ranging from elementary schools to high schools (O'Leary & O'Leary, 1977).

3) Soft reprimands. A soft reprimand is a reprimand that is audible only to the child being reprimanded. In contrast, a loud reprimand is a reprimand that is audible to the whole class. Loud reprimands are certainly the most frequent type

of reprimands, and they are easier to deliver because a teacher can give such a reprimand from any place in the classroom. In contrast, a soft reprimand has to be given near the child, so that movement around the class is necessary. Soft reprimands have proven very useful with children who have problems of aggression and hyperactivity. They are more effective than loud ones when combined with praise—as they should be. Soft reprimands initially require considerable effort, but they are so effective in reducing undesired behavior that eventually much less effort is required because fewer and fewer reprimands need to be given. In addition, when using soft reprimands, a teacher is seen more positively by his or her pupils than when using loud reprimands. Of course, occasional reprimands will have to be given to children in any classroom, but they generally should be avoided.

4) Rules. The teacher's classroom rules should be made clear to all children, and these rules should be posted where all children can see them. Such posting and even occasional review of the rules is highly desireable at the beginning of the school year. Posting and review of rules does not *necessarily* lead to any reduction in undesired behavior, but knowledge of rules makes it easier for children to ascertain what is expected of them.

5) Daily goals. A teacher can discuss daily goals with the child and give the child intermittent feedback about progress toward such goals. Setting specific daily goals of an academic and social nature helps a child know what is expected in terms he or she can readily understand. Goal setting on a daily basis also prompts a teacher to give the child frequent feedback about his or her performance. Goals should be attainable, and changed when reached consistently.

6) Feedback to parents. Sometimes a child is not very responsive to teacher attention and praise, but is likely to respond to parent attention. With proper consultation, par-

ents can be prompted to consistently praise and reward desired academic and social behavior. Examples of rewards for desired academic behavior that have been effective include extra television time, a special dessert, a game with a parent, or a family outing of the child's choice.

The daily feedback system often involves a daily report card submitted by the teacher to parents like the one below.

Daily Report Card

Date _____ Name of Child _____

	Yes	No
1. Finished math assignment by 10:00 a.m.	_____	_____
2. 80 percent correct on spelling	_____	_____
3. Got in line without pushing	_____	_____
Reward earned	_____	_____
Teacher's signature _____		

Feedback to parents can sometimes backfire, however, if the child frequently obtains negative evaluations by the teacher and/or if the parent is generally punitive. As a routine practice, I conduct a detailed interview with both the parents and child regarding disciplinary practices before implementing a daily feedback system. If parents are highly punitive, a daily feedback system should be avoided or carefully monitored.

Programs using the above procedures in classrooms have been effective with both hyperactive and aggressive children (O'Leary & O'Leary, 1977). These procedures have been experimentally validated both in isolation and as total programs. However, with relatatively serious behavior problems in school, professional consultation should be sought. There are causes of such behavior that lie outside the classroom, and the burden of changing the child's behavior should not fall on the teacher alone. The child, parents, and the teacher should work together with professional consultation to change the child's behavior, if possible. In turn, it will usually be seen that changes in teacher and parent behavior are also in order.

Behavior therapy programs designed to change the cognitive strategies of aggressive children have been designed by investigators like Camp (1977), who taught children to ask themselves the following questions: What is my problem? What is my plan? Am I using my plan? and How did I do? To teach the children to verbalize the cognitive strategy, a teacher asked the children to play "copycat" and repeat the questions after the teacher. Later, the child was taught to verbalize the strategies to him or herself when encountering a social or academic problem. The children also were taught a problem-solving strategy which included recognizing emotions of others, predicting outcomes in interpersonal situations, and evaluating the fairness of the outcomes.

The Camp training program involved six weeks of daily training with specially-trained teachers. To facilitate the use of the training procedures in the classroom, the children were asked to use the problem-solving strategy to complete their school work or to deal with problems with others. Aggressive children who received the program were compared with aggressive children who did not receive such a program. The experimental program was associated with improvement on laboratory measures often used to assess aggressive children's behavior. More specifically, the children were less impulsive and more accurate in completing mazes (a measure of impulsivity). Unfortunately, teacher ratings of aggression in the classroom did not indicate any significant improvement by the children who received the training. Nonetheless, programs to change children's self-control and cognitive strategies can be especially useful if combined with consultation with parents and teachers about behavior management (Douglas, 1979).

Psychotherapy

Psychotherapy is a form of therapy that relies upon discussion and insight into the causes of a problem for production of change in behavior. Such therapy has been quite effective with adult depression and anxiety and fears (Sloane, Staples, Cristol, Yorkston, & Whipple, 1975). Good verbal and cognitive ability is necessary for psychotherapy to be effective. More specifically, a child must be able to develop insight *and* be able to transfer this insight into the problematic situation. For example, when a child faces a problem such as being teased by other children, the child has to remember the solution discussed with the therapist and utilize the solution in the face of an emotional difficulty. Young children may be able to give the therapist a very good solution to a problem when the child and therapist are discussing the problem in an office, but under stress aggressive children often fail to remember the rational solutions. Older children (ages 8 to 12) and adolescents who have average intelligence can often profit from discussion of their problems and ways to solve them, and I always involve such children in the search for solutions to their problems. When psychotherapy is combined with a therapist's consultation with parents, and when teachers and parents use consequences for behavior, psychotherapy can be effective and, I think, highly desireable. On the other hand, psychotherapy alone has not proven effective with hyperactive and aggressive children (Love, Kaswan, & Bugental, 1972; Wender & Wender, 1978).

One form of psychotherapy used with children is play therapy, which has been called a method of helping problem children to help themselves (Axline, 1978). It involves regular visits by the child to the therapist and play therapy room, during which the child is free to play with the play materials, talk, or do whatever he or she chooses. The only limitations established by the therapist are those necessary to insure the protection and safety of the play materials, room, child, and therapist. The therapist reflects the child's feelings back to the child, and strives always to convey respect, understanding, and acceptance to the child. Proponents of play therapy believe that when the child feels completely accepted by the therapist, the conditions for self-growth have been established, and under these conditions the child will discover more satisfying, mature types of behavior. That is, the child is believed to be capable of positive self-growth when he or she feels accepted. According to play therapists, it is not necessary for the child to realize he or she has a problem before he or she can benefit from this type of therapy, nor is it necessary for parents to be helped in concomitant therapy. If the child has social problems, play therapy may be offered with a small group of other children. There is no existing evidence that play therapy is effective with hyperactive and aggressive children, and I cannot recommend such therapy.

Psychotherapists of a psychodynamic orientation stress current parent-child conflicts and the development of personality factors of the child in the preschool years. There is little clear evidence that such psychotherapy works if the therapy is conducted solely with the child, but if parents are involved in a child's treatment, the therapy may be quite useful. Although there are different psychotherapy orientations, among therapists who have ten years of experience or more, there is often great similarity in terms of what they actually do with the child and his or her parents. More specifically, most therapists first try to understand the child's problems by having detailed interviews with the parents and child about the child's social and emotional development. Frequently, tests or rating scales are used to gain additional information about the child. Then treatment will begin with some combination of sessions for the parents and child. Psychodynamic therapists usually focus on the child's early developmental history and the relationship established between the child and the therapist. In contrast, the behavior therapist will spend somewhat more time on recent history of current problems and relationships between the child and his parents and teachers. Good clinicians usually combine the best of all interventions, and, as will be noted in the last chapter of this book, the personality and reputation of the therapist is generally as important as any label of the therapist's theoretical orientation. In fact, most mental health professionals do not list their orientation in health directories or telephone books; rather, they simply identify themselves as a psychologist, psychiatrist, or social worker.

Tutoring (educational therapy). Most children who are eleven years old or older who have serious problems of aggression and hyperactivity also have academic deficiencies. That is, these children often have spent time daydreaming, disrupting others, and fooling around in classrooms while their peers were attending and learning. I am not implying that children should be blamed for their academic problems, but simply pointing out that these children have been in school for several years and have not profited academically as well as others from the school experience. Hyperactive children do not attend well, and aggressive children often do not have the frustration tolerance necessary to stay at an academic task for as long as their classmates typically can. Because of either one or both of these problems (short attention span and low frustration tolerance), extra academic help is usually necessary for the child. Also, an improvement academically may lead to an improvement behaviorally.

Sometimes a parent may have the extra time and patience necessary to help the child. In many instances, however, extra tutorial help from the school or from private tutors is necessary. In my experience, such tutoring is most helpful when the tutor is aware of the child's particular educational program and can use books from the child's regular classes. When a tutor uses the regular materials, the child can see some direct benefit from the tutorial aid. Further, there is no need to rely on generalized transfer from one set of educational materials to another.

The problem of transfering skills from one setting to another is a serious one which parents should keep in mind when seeking help for an academic problem. Some educational therapies rely on training motor and perceptual skills, but these skills (e.g., tracing, walking a balance beam, tracking a light, fixating on an object) do not transfer directly to academic skill. More specifically, if a child learns to trace patterns well or learns to track objects visually, he or she may or may not be able to read and write better. There are instances in which a child may need professional help for visual and motor problems, but I repeat that parents should not expect academic improvement to result directly from such professional help. There is some evidence that visual training exercises themselves will lead to improved reading (Arnold, Barnebry, McManus, Smeltzer, Conrad, Winer, & Desgranges, 1977), but such results are certainly not always the case. Direct academic tutoring is often the only way such improvement will occur. If it is expected that visual and/or motor problems interfere with a child's academic progress, professional consultation regarding visual problems and educational tutoring should be sought. Finally, it should be recognized that psychostimulant medication can lead to enhanced motor coordination, and children who have difficulty printing or writing show remarkable improvement with such medication.

Guidelines for Parents

Responsibility for behavior. Often, parents of a hyperactive child feel that the child behaves the way he/she does because of a physical or biochemical abnormality. Minimal brain dysfunction and genetic predispositions to hyperactivity are discussed in professional journals and popular magazines as causes for the child's problems. Even if such physical or biochemical problems are partly responsible for some children's problems, there is absolutely no evidence that biochemical or brain abnormalities can be seen as the only reason for such behavior. As parents, you must behave as if the child is partly responsible for his or her behavior. As Wender and Wender (1978) very aptly pointed out in discussing responsibility and accountability for behavior, "the child should not be held to be either irresponsible or blameworthy. He should be treated as someone who has a greater tendency than average to do certain things" (p. 67). They also go on to point out that some of a hyperactive child's behavior may not be responsive to parents' attempts at discipline. For example, they note that it may be easier to teach a hyperactive child how to take responsibility for chores than to teach him or her to have a longer attention span. While the hyperactive behavior of some children and the aggressive behavior of others may be due to physical or biochemical problems, they can have some control over their own behavior, and they must be held partly responsible for their actions.

Praise of appropriate behavior. As you have seen in the description of behavior therapy programs for both school and home, praise and other forms of positive attention for desired behavior are crucial elements of the programs. All of us are dependent upon positive events to motivate us and to maintain our behavior, and hyperactive and aggressive children need such feedback even more than we do. They need such positive feedback because they so frequently experience criticism and failure—especially regarding their school experience.

Parents and teachers often find themselves feeling angry toward children with problems of hyperactivity and aggression; I have seen hundreds of parents who become so frustrated that they resort to incessant verbal punishment and sometimes to physical abuse. Nonetheless, it is only by positive means that we can teach a child to do something that he or she will continue to do on his or her own in our absence. When you praise a child, it may even require you to act more positively than you sometimes feel. You cannot fool a child for long, but acting more positively than you feel for a short time will often enable a parent to change a negative atmosphere to a positive one. It is wise to praise a child as soon as possible after the good behavior. Immediate rewards are usually more effective than delayed rewards. However, if you give a child a reason for the praise, you can be effective even if your praise occurs sometime after the desired behavior. For example, you might say, "I was very glad to hear from Mrs. Jones that you behaved well on the school bus this week and that you were polite." Finally, it is very important to make the praise as specific as possible. That is, it is not as helpful to say, "You did a very good job cleaning your room today" as to say, "You cleaned your room very well today. You picked up all your clothes and put them in the closet, you cleaned off your dresser, and you made your bed." The more specific you make the feedback, the more helpful it will be to the child because he or she will know specifically what you like. It will also communicate to the child that you noticed every aspect of his or her good behavior.

Listen to a child's feelings. Children, like adults, need to be understood. Further, they want to feel understood by someone who is important to them, such as their teacher, parents, or grandparents (Ginott, 1973; Wender & Wender, 1978). Hyperactive and aggressive children experience more frustration and criticism than the average child, and it is very helpful for a parent to listen to a child's feelings about his or her day. Often, young school-age children are not very adept at expressing their feelings, but you can help them by patiently listening and encouraging them to talk. Restate the child's feelings to show him or her that you are listening closely and you understand. The child may tell you about an event in which he or she acted inappropriately, so it is very important to remember to listen without criticism. Listen first; provide feedback later! Otherwise you will teach a child not to tell you about problems that he or she has. Finally, even if you do not get to the point where a child understands what you think he or she should have done, a child will usually feel relieved (less tense and less angry) after telling someone about a problem he or she had. In summary, listening to a child express his/her feelings will help you understand the child, and it will provide a child with an often-needed release of emotions.

Summary

Psychological treatments for hyperactive and aggressive children consist mainly of behavior therapy and psychodynamically-oriented psychotherapy. Behavior therapy is the application of learning principles in the treatment of psychological, educational, and social problems. Psychotherapy is the use of discussion and insight in the treatment of psychological problems. The effectiveness of behavior therapy with hyperactive and aggressive children is relatively well-established in both the home and school. Psychodynamically-oriented psychotherapy has not been shown to be effective with the children's problems we have been discussing in this book. However, many experienced clinicians combine elements of behavior therapy and psychotherapy, and the personality and reputation of the particular therapist is often more important than the label of his or her therapeutic approach. Educational tutoring is often a necessity for hyperactive and aggressive children because they usually have academic deficiencies. While many approaches to tutoring exist, it is wise to seek help which focuses directly on exercises from the child's classroom. For some children with severe motor coordination and attentional problems, medication and perceptual training may be a necessity.

Three general rules were discussed for parents:

1) A child must be seen at least partly responsible for his/her own behavior.

2) Praise and other forms of positive feedback are the crucial elements in almost any psychological treatment, and it should be immediate and specific.

3) Listen to your child's feelings. By listening, you will understand your child better and help your child feel loved and important.

References

Alexander, J. F. and Parsons, B. V. Short term behavioral intervention with delinquent families: Impact on family process and recidivism. *Journal of Abnormal Psychology*, 1973, *81*, 219–225.

Arnold, L., Barnebry, N., McManus, J., Smeltzer, D., Conrad, A., Winer, G., Desgranges, L. Prevention by specific perceptual remediation for vulnerable first graders. *Archives of General Psychiatry*, 1977, *34*, 1279–1294.

Axline, V. *Play Therapy*, Boston: Houghton Mifflin, 1947.

Camp, B. W. Verbal mediation in young aggressive boys. *Journal of Abnormal Psychology*, 1977, *86*, 145–153.

Douglas, V. I. Treatment and training approaches to hyperactivity: Establishing internal or external control. In C. K. Whalen and B. Henker (Eds.) *Hyperactive Children: The Social Ecology of Identification and Treatment*, 1980. Academic Press, New York.

Dubey, D.R., O'Leary, S. G., and Kaufman, K. F. Training parents of hyperactive children in child management: A comparative outcome study. *Journal of Abnormal Child Psychology*, 1983, *11*, 229–246.

Foster, S. L., Prinz, R. J., and O'Leary, K. D. Impact of problem-solving communication training and generalization procedures on family conflict. *Child Behavior Therapy*, 1983, *5*, 1–23.

Ginott, H. *Between Parent and Child: New Solutions to Old Problems*. MacMillan, New York, 1973.

Love, L. R., Kaswan, J. K., Bugental, D. E. Differential effectiveness of three clinical interventions for different socioeconomic groupings, *Journal of Consulting and Clinical Psychology*, 1972, *39*, 347–360.

Madsen, C., Becker, W., and Thomas, D. Rules, praise, and ignoring: Elements of elementary classroom control. *Journal of Applied Behavior Analysis*, 1968, *1*, 139–150.

O'Leary, K. D., and O'Leary, S. G. *Classroom Management: The Successful Use of Behavior Modification* (revised with new readings and commentaries). New York: Pergamon Press, 1977.

Patterson, G. R. and Fleischman, M. J. Maintenance of treatment effects: Some considerations concerning family systems and follow-up data. *Behavior Therapy*, 1979, *10*, 168–185.

Patterson, G. R. and Guillion, M. E. *Living with Children: New Methods for Parents and Teachers*, Champaign, Illinois: Research Press, 1968.

Patterson, G. R., Reid, J. B., Jones, R. R., and Conger, R. E. *A Social Learning Approach to Family Intervention, Vol. 1, Families with Aggressive Children*. Eugene, Oregon: Castalia Publishing Co., 1975.

Sloane, R. B., Staples, R. R., Cristol, A. H., Yorkston, N. H., and Whipple, K. *Psychotherapy versus behavior therapy*. Cambridge, Massachusetts: Harvard University Press, 1975.

Wender, P. H. and Wender, E. H. *The Hyperactive Child and the Learning Disabled Child*, Crown Publishers, Inc., New York, 1978.

Where Can I Get Help?

Help Must Start at Home

In an interview study of adolescents and young adults who were formerly diagnosed as hyperactive as young children, the adolescents said the most important source of help in their lives was their mother (Weiss, Hectman, Perlman, Hopkins & Wener, 1979). More specifically, they said the most important source of aid to them as a hyperactive child had been "a mother who believed in my potential for success." The second most important source of help to them was "a teacher who recognized my worth." In brief, while you will certainly want to seek professional help if you have a child with serious problems of over-activity and aggression, it should be re-emphasized that a parents' faith in a child appears to be a very important factor in a child's success. This message should be kept in mind no matter what professional is sought or how much professional help is received.

Who Recognizes or Labels Behavior as Problematic?

Usually the teacher is the first person to talk to parents about their child's problems. This pattern is quite reasonable when we realize that aggression and hyperactivity are most obvious in situations that require continued attention and ability to delay gratification. If the teacher is concerned that the problem is serious and is not improving, he or she may request an evaluation of the child by the school psychologist, a clinical psychologist, the family physician, or a pediatrician.

Of course, as parents read more books and magazine articles about problems of aggression and hyperactivity, they fortunately often seek professional consultation on their own. In such instances, I often encounter greater motivation to deal with the

117

problem than when the parents feel pushed into seeing me or someone else for help regarding the problem. Fortunately, the opinions of parents and teachers are often very similar, and even when a parent decides there is a problem to be addressed by a professional, the parent often will find it extremely useful to talk to the teacher. The teacher is generally the individual who knows a child better than anyone outside the family.

Which Professional Should I Talk With?

There are some professionals who feel they should always be consulted. For example, Drs. Paul and Esther Wender (1978), physicians specializing in the pediatric and psychitaric areas, both stated the following:

"We wish to emphasize that in either case [whether problems related to hyperactivity are recognized by teachers, guidance counselors, psychologists, or parents themselves] in order to ascertain the probable sources of the child's difficulties, the parents *must* consult a physician who is knowledgeable about the entire range of children's physical and emotional problems, including hyperactivity." (p. 129)

I see no reason why any one professional should be sought always or first. My own opinion is that most problems of aggression and hyperactivity of children in regular or normal schools are best addressed by child psychologists. Very often, it is also necessary to obtain special tutoring to increase the child's academic achievement. However, as we discussed in the chapter, "Physiological and Biological Causes of Aggression and Hyperactivity," there are certain cases that clearly require a physician's attention. For example, if gross neurological problems are suspected because of birth complications, some head injury in childhood, or some physical illness that caused a very high fever, a medical evaluation is in order. Further, it is always advisable to consult a physician for a physical examination if such an examination has not been obtained within the past year.

In some communities where professional help is scarce, it is probably best to inquire from various sources about the person who is best suited to coordinate a diagnostic and treatment plan. In certain instances, the pediatrician or psychiatrist may be the best professional to coordinate such a plan, whereas in other instances, a child psychologist may be best for the task. In all cases, one must find an individual who is willing to pursue various leads and make contact with varied professionals. Most importantly, one may inquire about the education, personality, and professional interests of the specialist.

Education of professional. First, one can ask when and where the professional obtained his or her training. More importantly, one will want to find out whether the person received specialized training in childhood problems. A psychiatrist or psychologist who was trained in the treatment of adult problems is not the preferred person to see. Problems of hyperactive and aggressive children are not simply problems of adults on a small scale; they are entirely different problems.

If you assume that a professional received his or her professional training a long time ago, (e.g., If you know the professional is between 40 and 65, it would be a good bet that he or she received professional training fifteen to thirty years ago), it is imperative to obtain some sense of whether the individual updates himself or herself on recent research in diagnosis and treatment. There have been, and will continue to be, many fads in the treatment of hyperactivity and aggression, and one needs a professional whose knowledge is current. In a few states in the United States there are requirements for continuing education for physicians and psychologists to maintain their licenses to practice in their disciplines. However, such requirements do not exist in most states or most places in the world. If the professional is associated with a university or professional center, he or she is likely to be well-informed regarding recent developments in the field, although it is not necessarily the case that such individuals are better *practitioners.*

Personality of the professional. One can best learn about the personality of a professional from former patients or clients. Flexibility, patience, friendliness, and warmth are key factors in the treatment of an aggressive or hyperactive child. The professional must have the flexibility to deal effectively with the child, parents, and varied professionals. As should be obvious to you from reading this book, the problems of a hyperactive or aggressive child generally are not ones that change very rapidly, with or without professional aid. Thus, patience is a key virtue of the professional who should provide supportive consultation to parents regarding the likely course and outcome of the treatment. Friendliness and warmth are critical factors in treating children; the professional must know how to relate well with children if the child is to cooperate with treatment efforts. Developing a good relationship with a child requires a sensitivity to the child's feelings and a knowledge of how to gain the child's trust.

Interests of the professional. It is worthwhile to inquire in your community about the professionals who have an interest in the problems of childhood aggression and hyperactivity. Generally, when a person has a special interest in such a problem, he or she will do a very good job in treating the problem. However, there are exceptions. For example, there are professionals whose patients or children received help from a particular method, and they subsequently may ignore all other methods, continuing to use only one method, even when it may not be appropriate.

Let us now turn to a description of the various professionals who provide aid to families with children who have problems of aggression and hyperactivity.

Psychologists. A clinical psychologist is an individual who has completed four to five years of graduate training, a clinical internship, and has received a Ph.D. In order to practice privately, the clinical psychologist must be licensed or certified in the particular state in which he or she practices. A clinical child psychologist specializes in child and family problems. Most clinical psychologists are trained in problems of learning and motivation, and some are trained in specialized assessment of learning disabilities.

School Psychologists. School psychologists generally have masters degrees in psychology, with a specialization in problems of children in school settings. In large school districts, a school psychologist may have a Ph.D. in school psychology and supervise other masters-level psychologists. School psychologists can be very helpful in the assessment and diagnosis of learning problems and in the assessment of the school atmosphere as it bears upon particular children. More specifically, school psychologists are often best equipped to assess learning disabilities, intelligence, and perceptual-motor problems. Some clinical child psychologists are also well equipped to assess such problems, but school psychologists spend the majority of their time testing children and are thus very well attuned to local factors as they influence test performance (e.g., cultural biases, whether a child might score poorly simply because of lack of experience with a particular set of concepts).

Social Workers. Social workers often have college training and postgraduate education (Master's Degree) or sometimes doctorates in social work (D.S.W.). The daily roles of social workers vary greatly from country to country. However, there is a tradition long-established by social workers of helping families secure aid for food, housing and health care from government sources. In some countries social workers also do individual counseling and psychotherapy, and social workers often complete the initial interviews with families in schools, mental health clinics and hospitals.

Family medicine practitioners. These individuals are physicians who have completed four years of medical school (M.D.), and a one-year internship. In addition, some family medicine physicians have completed three-year residencies. Family practitioners deal with a wide variety of medical problems experienced by any member in a family; they provide care for a wide variety of problems of both children and adults. They tend to know where individuals should be referred for problems that require the attention of varied specialists in medicine, psychology, and education. As is the case for all M.D.s, they can prescribe medication.

Pediatricians. A pediatrician is a physician (M.D.) who has completed medical school, an internship, and a three-year residency in pediatrics. The pediatrician is trained to diagnose and treat a wide variety of childhood diseases. However, now that many of the fatal childhood diseases have been conquered with vaccination programs, pediatricians are receiving more training in disease prevention, nutrition, and behavioral problems.

Neurologists. A neurologist is a physician (M.D.) who has completed medical school, an internship, and a three-year residency in neurology. Neurologists are trained to diagnose and treat problems of children, including gross dysfunctions of the nervous system associated with metabolic disorders.

Psychiatrists. A psychiatrist is a physician (M.D.) who has completed medical school, an internship, and a residency in psychiatry. Psychiatrists specialize in emotional, behavioral, and mental problems, and they often specialize in pharmacological (drug) treatment of certain disorders. Other psychiatrists specialize in psychotherapy of various forms.

Educators. The teachers, both in regular and special classes, have been the persons given too little attention in the treatment of children with problems of aggression and hyperactivity. Perhaps the reason for this neglect is that educators have not developed educational programs particularly designed for children with the problems in question. More specifically, they have not designed tutorial programs that are specially tailored to the problems of hyperactive or aggressive children. However, as we discussed earlier, a focus on the child's educational problems is an absolute necessity in most cases.

Elementary school teacher. A child's elementary school teacher usually has the first opportunity to view a child in a structured situation where the child must comply with rules and share the attention of the adult (teacher) with many other children. A teacher with a few years of experience generally has interacted with at least 100 children of the same age and he or she is in a good position to compare a child to others with similar backgrounds. As importantly, teachers have more contact with a child than any other adult outside the family and they are in a position to observe daily fluctuations in behavior that may be associated with home problems, dietary changes, or medication changes. In brief, the child's teacher is often a key person in any treatment problem.

Special class teachers. Sometimes a child may be placed in a special class because of emotional and/or behavioral problems. Special class teachers may be trained to teach children who are brain injured or emotionally disturbed. Such teaching may require that a child be taught in a way that the child's assets are used to his or her fullest potential (e.g., for a child who has an ability to learn by hearing but has difficulty reading, the material might be presented in spoken form as much as possible). Special materials and learning devices are often especially helpful in this regard.

Issues in choosing any professional. Any professional who provides help to parents and a child should be able to provide the following information: (1) how much the treatment program will cost and how long the program will likely last, (2) where another professional's opinion can be obtained, and (3) what their own credentials are and what training in treating childhood problems he or she has had.

Helping Ourselves. In the long run, the persons who are likely to have most impact on a child with conduct problems are his/her parents. In the chapter on diagnosis I discussed how a psychologist uses information parents provide to decide whether a child should receive professional treatment. You can use that information yourself to get an idea of whether your child would be advised to receive help from a professional. However, whether it is decided your child needs such help or not, as a parent you will undoubtedly want to aid your child—either to reduce existing problems or to prevent future problems.

One of the first steps in changing a child's behavior is to record the behaviors you wish to increase and decrease, as well as the events surrounding the behavior. Of course you can change behavior without recording the behavior, but you are likely to be much more successful in the long run if you take the time to count the behaviors of interest. Your record system need not be elaborate, but it should be specific, and your records should be kept daily. For example, you could simply use a 5 × 7 index card on which you keep the following information:

	Behavior	Events Before	Events After
Sun	Bob hit brother, John	John refused to give him an apple	John cried
	No hitting	---	---
Mon			
	Bob hit brother	John was calling him "Fatty"	John told his Dad about the teasing
Tues			
	Bob hit brother	Nothing unusual	John cried
Wed			
	No hitting	---	---
Thurs			
	No hitting	---	---
Fri			
	No hitting	---	---
Sat			

Behaviors you wish to decrease are recorded along with the events that can provide insight into some of the reasons for Bob's aggression. A week of recording is not long enough to give one a good idea of the factors that lead to the problem behavior, but several weeks of such recording helps a great deal.

Larger events in the household which affect your child, e.g., a fight between husband and boss, husband and wife, death of pet, unusual frustration at school, may also be noted. In addition, behaviors to be increased should be kept on a separate card so that all family attention is not focused on negative aspects of a child. For example, the record below reveals that parents are not supportive of the very behaviors they desire.

	Behavior	Events Before	Events After
Mon.	Took out garbage	Father told him to take out garbage	Nothing
Tues	---	---	---
Wed	Set table	Mother left him a note to set table before she got home	Mother praised him at supper for setting table
Thurs	Set table	Note from mother	Nothing
Fri	---	---	---
Sat	Did lawn	Told by father to mow lawn—"We all have responsibilities"	---
Sun	---	---	---

As can be seen from the week's records, the child is being ignored for 75 percent of the desired behavior (3 out of 4 desired behaviors). Just as we adults need support and encouragement, our children need such encouragement too. We need to reward improvements, and even though we may want more "good" behavior from our children, we must start where they are and progress from that point. If we wait until we see nearly 100 percent of what we desire, we may never obtain any change.

Parents can do many things to bring about change in their children, and a number of these things were outlined in the chapter on psychological treatments. Further, a list of specific self-help manuals was provided for you. However, some general rules for helping your child change are as follows:

1. Model the kind of behavior yourself that you want to see in your child. (Children Do As We Say, Not As We Do!)
2. Make your house rules and expectations clear.
3. Encourage desired behavior with praise and affection.
4. Punish as infrequently as possible, and when you do, don't lecture. Most children just tune their parents out when they do this.

5. Listen carefully to your child's reactions to school, friends, and relatives.
6. Give your child reasons for your actions and help him or her see reasons for behaving in certain ways. For example, tell him or her the specific reasons he or she was rewarded or punished.

Use of these six guidelines can often have very beneficial results without the use of any professional consultation. Best of luck in your application of them.

References for Parents and Teachers

In order to alert parents and teachers to specific reference sources which may be helpful in choosing an approach in selecting a particular professional, and in implementing certain treatments, a list of references is provided at the end of this book.

Summary

Adolescents and young adults who were formerly hyperactive feel that their mother was their most important source of help to them. Their teachers were their next most valuable source of help. In brief, parents and teachers who convey that they believe that children can succeed and who provide positive feedback to the children can be very important. In seeking help from a professional outside the school, it is important to know what the person's area of expertise is, and it is certainly fitting to ask about his or her qualifications. However, of key importance is the professional's personality and his or her ability to get along with both children and adults. When you consult a professional, you should find out how long the therapeutic or educational program will last.

No matter how much consultation a parent receives from a professional, in the long run, the parent will have to provide the child with daily support and guidance, and general rules for helping your child change are:
1. Model the behavior yourself that you want to see in your child.

2. Make your house rules and expectations clear.
3. Encourage desired behavior with praise and affection.
4. Punish as infrequently as possible.
5. Listen carefully to your child's reactions to school, friends, and relatives.
6. Give your child reasons for your actions.

References

Weiss, G., Hechtman, L., Perlman, T., Hopkins, J., & Wener, A. Hyperactives as young adults. *Archives of General Psychiatry*, 1979, *36*, 675–681.

Wender, P. H., and Wender, E. H., *The Hyperactive Child and the Learning Disabled Child*, Crown Publishers, Inc., New York, 1978.

Books About Aggressive Children for Parents

Behavioral treatments
Patterson, G. R., Reid, J., Jones, R., & Conger, R. *Families with aggressive children: A social learning approach to family intervention, 1975*. Research Press, 2612 North Mattis Avenue, Champaign, Illinois, 61820.

Books for Parents About Hyperactive Children

Dietary treatments
Connors, C. K. *Food additives and hyperactive children*, 1980. Plenum Press, 227 West 17th Street, New York, New York 10011. Also published in London.
Pharmacological treatments
Wender, P. H., & Wender, E. H. *The hyperactive child and the learning disabled child*, 1978. Crown Publishers, Inc., One Park Avenue, New York, New York 10016. (Published in Canada by General Publishing Co. Limited).
Safer, D. J., & Allen, R. P. *Hyperactive children: Diagnosis and management*, 1976. University Park Press, Chamber of Commerce Building, Baltimore, Maryland 21202. (This book was written for professionals, but it is an excellent source book for both pharmacological and behavioral management).
Behavioral treatments and behavioral management in the home (For Parents)
Stewart, M. A., & Olds, S. W. *Raising a hyperactive child*, 1973. Harper & Row, Inc., 10 East 53rd Street, New York, New York 10022. Published in Canada by Fitzhenry & Whiteside.
Patterson, G. R. *Families: Applications of social learning to family life*, 1977. Research Press, 2612 North Mattis Avenue, Champaign, Illinois 61820.
Becker, W. C. *Parents are teachers: A child management program*, 1971. Research Press, 2612 North Mattis Avenue, Champaign, Illinois 61820.

Books for Teachers about Hyperactive and Aggressive Children

Pharmacological treatments
Gadow, K. D. *Children on medication: A primer for school personnel,* 1979. The Council for Exceptional Children, 1920 Association Drive, Reston, Virginia 22091.

Behavioral treatments in the classroom (For Teachers)
Buckley, N. K., & Walker, H. M. *Modifying classroom behaviors: A manual of procedures for classroom teachers,* 1970. Research Press, 2612 North Mattis Avenue, Champaign, Illinois 61820.

O'Leary, K. D., & O'Leary, S. G. *Classroom management: The successful use of behavior modification* (2nd ed.), 1979. Pergamon Press, Fairview Park, Elmsford, New York 10523.

Sulzer-Azaroff, G., & Mayer, G. R. *Applying behavior analysis procedures with children and youth,* 1977. Holt, Rinehart, & Winston, New York, New York.

Madsen, C. H., Jr., & Madsen, C. K. *Teaching/discipline: Behavioral principles toward a positive approach,* 1974. Allyn & Bacon, 470 Atlantic Avenue, Boston, Massachusetts.

INDEX

PARENTS COLLECTION

DATE